Barry Brickell

A HEAD OF STEAM

BARRY BRICKELL

A HEAD OF STEAM

CHRISTINE LEOV-LEALAND

NEW ZEALAND LIVES: THE PEOPLE WHO SHAPED THE NATION

Exisle Publishing Ltd
PO Box 8077, Auckland, New Zealand.

Series Editor: Tim Chamberlain.
Founding Editor: Roger Robinson.

Designed by Craig Humberstone.
Typeset in Berkeley, Trajan and Helvetica by
Streamline Graphic Imaging Ltd, Auckland.

ISBN 0-908988-08-7

Printed by Colorcraft Ltd, Hong Kong.

*(Front Cover) Barry Brickell raising steam at Driving Creek, August 1995 (photograph: Tim Chamberlain).
(Frontispiece) The world of Barry Brickell (montage by Heather Ball from photographs by Tim
Chamberlain, Marti Friedlander, Steve Rumsey and Bob Stott). (Back Cover) Driving Creek Railway
offers an intimate experience of nature, technology and art. Barry at the controls of The Snake trainset
(photograph: Tim Chamberlain).*

For Terence P Lealand
With thanks for the gifts of Monkey.

ACKNOWLEDGEMENTS

My sincerest thanks go to the following people who have been of invaluable assistance to me in my researches:

Barry Brickell, Deirdre Airey, Duncan Bayne, Nancy Beck, David Black, Derek Brickell, Romilly Brickell, Shirley and Maurice Brickell, Len Castle, John Smith-Dodsworth, Michael Draffin, Wailin Elliott, Janis Fairburn, Marti Friedlander, Tim Garrity, Jane Hamann, Denis and Joy Hanna, Jo Hardy, Rhys Hill, Peter Hughson, Kelvin Hynes, Kevin Ireland, Wilbert Keiller and family, Hamish Keith, Barry Lett, Henry Mackeson, Helen Mason, John and Lynda Matthews, Ruth McCallum, Lois McIvor, Peter McLeavey, Petra Meyboden, Peter Millington, John Money, Murray Norman, Claudia Reis, Elwyn Richardson, Steve Rumsey, Yvonne Rust, Jeff Scholes, Ray Scott, Mirek Smíšek, Mervyn Smith, Peter Tomory, Beran Whitcombe, Peter Yeates, Jocelyn Young.

Auckland University Library, Dowse Art Museum, Dunedin Art Gallery, John Leech Gallery, Manawatu Art Gallery, National Library of New Zealand, the Govett Brewster Art Gallery, the Hocken Library, the staff at Auckland Institute and Museum, the staff at Auckland City Art Gallery, and the Waikato Museum of Art and History.

Finally I would like to invite all who have helped at Driving Creek Railway and Pottery since 1961 in any way to contact me via Exisle Publishing, as I would like to make a list of those who have lived or worked there on both past and present sites.

For further information on pottery techniques and terms, see *A New Zealand Potter's Dictionary* by Barry Brickell.

CONTENTS

TIM CHAMBERLAIN

VISITORS please feel free To look around. my new Year's resolution is To Try To explain the objects and mysteries of This place. Notices like this are now pinned up ← . All I ask is that you respect our private areas (workshops, domestic places etc) and place litter in bins provided. Have a splendid new Year — Barry Brickell.

LIST OF ILLUSTRATIONS

RAISING STEAM

"Anatomically speaking, man has never devised a machine more like himself than the steam locomotive."   *– Barry Brickell*

Let us begin as Barry himself would begin a new project. "I will need sand under the wheels and will prepare my firebox for some very free steaming. In fact I shall rake out every last piece of clinker and ash, soot-blow my tubes, adjust the ring valve, fit a longer nozzle to my injector and prepare for business with a fittingly good head of steam. Ought one polish the whistle too? Perhaps this is too much so I might just settle for tube cleaning — a pleasant internal sensation especially when a red wire brush is used."

A glass of a good dry red wine is essential here to celebrate the life and the achievements to date of one of New Zealand's greatest potters and pioneers. A toast to Barry Brickell!

Poet Kevin Ireland describes Barry Brickell as "Potter, kiln builder, practical visionary, engineer, environmentalist, railway enthusiast, workaholic, amateur botanist, steam buff and helper of hundreds." All these epithets are accurate and have been embraced within the life of one extraordinary man.

My intention has been to investigate the truths and fictions about Barry Brickell, his life and works. I do not claim to be objective or exhaustive about my subject. It would take years of research and a much larger volume to include all those who have made a significant impact on his life and work.

I like to write without too much political bias about people and try to represent as honestly as possible what makes that person tick. Achieving this while the subject is still alive is no easy task. Fortunately Barry Brickell is still very much with us and I have had the privilege of working with him on this project. We sincerely hope you will celebrate with us and prepare for an enjoyable trip to Driving Creek Railway (DCR) and Pottery, past and present.

(Left) Barry Brickell is a fervent advocate of steam as an energy source. He hosts open days for members of the Auckland Steam Engine Society who fire up the old boilers with great enthusiasm.

PHOTOGRAPH: TIM CHAMBERLAIN

CHAPTER ONE

THE FIRE SETTER

"Fire is the ultimate form of animation." – Barry Brickell

"I think the worst thing he ever did . . . we had a big old villa in Devonport which was about three feet off the ground. One day I smelt a smell as though something were burning in the house, so I shot outside as I thought it had been an electrical fault or something.

"I noticed underneath the house what appeared to be a flame. Sure enough it *was* a flame. Barry and his sister had built a little brick kiln. It was his first kiln — purely and simply a square kiln; he was seven — and they had lit a fire in the darn thing. The flames were actually licking the floor! Of course that house was tinder dry and if I hadn't got out there... five minutes more would have seen that house go up in flames."

STEVE RUMSEY

(Left) From the family album. (Above) A lifelong fascination with fire: Barry with an early kiln, 1957.

Even today, 52 years later, Maurice Brickell is angry about the threat to the family caused by his elder son's pyromania.

"Flame is something which has *always* fascinated Barry," his mother Shirley Brickell recalls. "He was always a very thoughtful little boy. He took a long time to learn to talk. He didn't speak properly until he was about four, and I was told he was mentally retarded. I knew darn well he wasn't.

"He went to St Anne's Kindergarten and he was absolutely one-track minded. He would go into raptures over unfolding fern fronds and things in the garden which nobody else noticed — not kids at that age — they didn't. His sister Andrea was born when he was 15 months old and they became the 'terrible twins'. They did everything together, awful things!"

The family moved from Meadowbank in Auckland's eastern suburbs to Cheltenham Beach, Devonport, in 1942 when Barry was seven years old. Maurice and Shirley were convinced that Devonport was a wonderful place for children to grow up. Their second son Gavin was born four years after Andrea. It was wartime and three months after Gavin was born Maurice Brickell was sent to war in the meteorological division of the airforce. He was away for three years. During this lonely and stressful time Shirley Brickell started the first playcentre in Devonport to give the wives of the servicemen a break from fulltime child care. In the summer they would often have holidays on Waiheke Island where the children would play on the beach and catch fish.

Nancy Beck, who lived nearby, comments: "The Brickells were a family who allowed the children to grow up as they wanted — were not over-critical of them. The kids weren't different; they just did different things."

As the eldest, Barry did not have the supervision that the younger children had and was able to run wild on the beach, exploring North Head and the old brickworks at Devonport.

At the end of the war Romilly, the younger daughter of the family, was born. She remembers: "When I was a child I adored Barry. He was 13 years older than me. He used to take me as a small child on his bike to the Devonport gasworks — that was the best — he would let me look into the spy holes, show me the roaring red and white hot kilns. He had spent years exploring and we would go to the clay pits together."

Barry adds: "I remember being a loner, spending as much time as possible alone. Running around the mudflats naked, that kind of thing... climbing rock cliffs, bicycling out to bush patches, exploring Devonport. I do remember occasionally sharing it with my sister; when I had discovered something I wanted to show her, I'd take her. But I'm not a family type. Always wanted to be on my own.

"I went to Vauxhall Primary School where a Mr Upton, an innovative teacher, taught us pottery making on a bicycle chain wheel in Standard 6 [Form 2]. Mr Upton actually took me aside and talked to me about my interests, because no one shared my interests then. No one at all. I had to run away from the other children all the time. I didn't find anyone at all compatible to be with.

"My uncle Bob Brickell was studying botany at Auckland University when I was at Vauxhall School and he gave me a copy — I still have it — of Laing and Blackwell's *Plants of New Zealand*. So I would ride my bike to the nearest patch of real bush, a regenerating kauri forest at Greenhithe, halfway to Albany, and that is where I learnt what epiphytes were. At school we were asked to do an essay for an Arbour Day competition which I won because I knew how to describe native bush, of which nobody else had any idea, not even the teachers."

From an early age, Barry was devoted to native plants and even sought to grow them in his mother's traditional English garden in Devonport. As a conservationist, he was ahead of his time.

"I hated rose gardens, because they were so boring — a boring desert. I

TIM CHAMBERLAIN

Maurice and Shirley Brickell at home, Driving Creek, Coromandel, September 1995.

wanted to animate my mother's rose garden so I planted manuka seedlings in it. I found the best way to do this was to dig carefully around the manuka plant so it had a ball of clay around its roots and then transplant it into mother's garden and carefully smooth the soil around it so it looked like the manuka plant had always been there."

Nancy Beck recalled that the children used to laugh about Barry coming home from the Devonport tip which was then at Narrow Neck. His bike would be so loaded up with junk you couldn't see him, but you could hear him making locomotive noises, steam chuffing and whistle sounds as he pedalled along towards home at Tui Street.

Barry's mother would complain that the good shirts she bought him at Hallensteins were ruined by his cutting the sleeves out raggedly up to the armpit so he could get 'free arm movement'. Always pragmatic, Barry saw that clothes fulfilled no practical necessity in the warm Auckland climate and wore them as little as possible.

Cheltenham Beach was an ideal place to grow up and the Brickell children's lives were full of adventure. Barry's father built him a P class yacht and on one occasion Barry sailed single-handed to forbidden Rangitoto from Cheltenham. Severely admonished for this act of daring, he was banished from Rangitoto. He then explored the 'civilised' wonders of the Waitemata Harbour.

After the war, Maurice Brickell was employed to inspect isolated weather stations around New Zealand. He organised expeditions during the school holidays so he could take the whole family, or at least Andrea and Barry, with him to special places like Little Barrier Island and Cape Brett lighthouse.

Barry continues: "In 1949, during my third form year at Takapuna Grammar School, I started getting interested in using fire to bake clay. From earliest childhood days fire had fascinated me. My experiments with fires in tins started before we moved to Devonport and continued in an 'underground' manner away from the view of my rather authoritarian father.

"One afternoon after school when he arrived home unexpectedly early from his work at the weather office he caught me playing with a mixture of burning oil, woodchips and paper in old tins underneath the old kauri villa that was the family residence. I got bashed despite my efforts to explain that the flames were never allowed near the dry timber joists, only four feet up.

"After that I was given a garden patch by Mum (reluctantly consented to by Dad) away from the house. Here I was happy, rushing home after school to experiment with fire power. Making steam in contrived boilers was my first dash — only to learn the hard way about the powerful scalding effects of steam as well as its wonderful capacity to boil water, make a vacuum and drive model engines which I borrowed.

"It was rewarding to melt lead and watch fire burning fuels and the behaviour of the bricks and metals surrounding the fire. I remember feeling pity for the viscous fluxing incandescent surfaces of a brick baffle inside an oil-fired ship's boiler, withstanding such awful punishment."

Nearby was a fire enthusiast's paradise, the Devonport Gas Company's gas and brickworks: "A whole enchanting world of fire, architectural and engineering forms. Occasionally I plucked up courage to creep about this spectacular place despite the men's threats to clear out. One night a stoker found me high up on the charging floor of the gasworks vertical retorts. After an initial lecture he let me watch the highly spectacular charging of the white hot retorts with West Coast coking coal. The firebrick works behind the gasworks had two huge coke-fired kilns which I used to study in great detail, especially during the firings. The things that interested me were the structural aesthetics of furnace design and architecture and the essential stacks, flues, steelwork, grime, wear and tear, colours, corrosion, smells and of course the spectacle. Chopin's piano studies always came to mind as I glimpsed the shimmering white hot bricks inside the kilns. I was in seventh heaven."

Barry's experimental curiosity led him to attempt to recreate the gasworks at home on his garden plot. "I got a piece of pipe, plugged the end and put some coal in that piece of pipe like a gas retort, and put it into one of my fires, one of my furnaces, and it made a gas which came out like a dense smoke which I would light and burn as a flame. Then I made little condensers and all sorts of things for a miniature gasworks to get the tar out of it. I learned to make my own tar. I would distil coal and wood in retorts made from old pipes, drawing off the most amazingly rich odorous tars and gases and found out many wonderful things about distillation. The stinks accompanied me beyond the bathroom into the dining room and school room and I was again given a hard time.

"One day I thought I would make a blow pipe, so I filled a container with gas and blew down one tube and lit a match at the outlet tube. I thought I would blow, making a huge long flame. [He laughs] Of course what happened, as soon as I lit the match, it blew up out the other way into my mouth and face — took most of my hair off the front of my face!

"It was the boss of the brickworks, Mr Don Cooper, who gave me my first piece of prepared clay, with the ulterior motive to get rid of me. Soon I was not only making hundreds of miniature bricks but building my first kilns fired on coke sneaked out of the gasworks yard by night bicycle. My bicycle was quite a well designed 'looting machine'. At the gasworks and brickworks the night shift was no obstacle to me, I'd get into all the various places I could find, pinch — they had so much coke lying around, heaps they didn't know what to do with; I used to go and help myself to this waste coke all the time. I fired my kilns with that as well as Westport coal that was lying round in spills everywhere.

"As a teenager I became involved with railways. Travelling on them. In the weekends I would ride my bike over on the vehicular ferry from Devonport to Auckland and then I'd ride around the railway yards picking up lumps of coal which had fallen off locomotives -— bringing two sacks of coal back, one on my carrier on the back and one on the front of my bike. I'd take the coal back to my studio in Devonport and practise firing kilns with it."

Len Castle and Barry became close friends in the 1950s. Barry's grandmother and Len's mother met and introduced the two young men to each other in 1950 when Barry was 14. Shirley Brickell was trying to find an outlet for Barry's pyromania and the 'new' craft of pottery seemed just the solution, with the focus on firing your pots in a kiln when they were dry. Once he had access to a regular source of clay, Barry would go to bed and surreptitiously coil pots beside the bed in the pitch dark. In the morning his mother would notice that the pot hidden under or beside the bed had grown taller than it had been the previous night. He kept this habit through his student years, of pinching or coiling pots in bed at night, instead of reading or writing a diary or just sleeping. He really needed friends with like interests and luckily Len Castle had a similar fascination with fire, kilns and clay.

"I went with bated breath to meet Len Castle," Barry remembers. "He was a recently graduated science teacher, living with his parents at Westmere where, in their back garden, he had a large coal-fired downdraught saggar kiln and huge kick wheel under the house. I was very scared of him as I was just a schoolboy at the time."

Len recalls: "From the very first meeting with Barry I knew I had met an unusual person, to say the least. Barry and I talked about pots and fire and he

Kiln firing, Tui Street, Devonport, 1957. From left: Joy Hanna, Barry Brickell, Theo Schoon, John Kingston, Keith Patterson, Maurice Brickell.

told me about a deposit of clay on Takapuna racecourse. I went over to Devonport, met Mr and Mrs Brickell and saw Barry's workshop, then we went off to look at this clay deposit which was not far from a bicycle track on the edge of the racecourse. We dug a lot of clay there and over the next few months these clay pits tended to turn into mantraps. It was a very good clay and I used some of it for my first stoneware pots."

Barry met Len on the dock when he returned to Auckland in 1957 from his year studying pottery at St Ives with Bernard Leach. "Barry was a very keen correspondent, I was less so," he says. "He used to send across drawings of kilns he had designed. He has a very good brain in terms of engineering problems, and these had ingenious methods built in of recapturing the excess heat and recirculating it and I used to be bombarded regularly with these plans with notes appended to the bottom of them. I'm rather sorry now that I have lost those plans because some of them were quite splendid."

From this time onward, Bernard Leach became Barry's 'God' of pottery techniques but it wasn't until 1962, when the English ceramicist visited New Zealand for the first time, that the two met.

Barry and Len remained close for many years, at times co-tutoring summer schools. Eventually, because of his holiday job as groundsman at the Adult Education Centre, Barry met Ruth Main, a weaving tutor, and introduced Len to his future wife. The other early potters Barry got to know were Patricia Perrin, Peter Stitchbury, Olive Jones, Neil Robertson, Ian Firth and Peter Webb ["who were working together making slip-cast ornamentalia"]. Also slip-casting were Selwyn Hadfield and Cameron Brown.

Kevin Ireland, who was three years ahead of Barry at Takapuna Grammar, describes Barry. "As I first remember him — a Devonport schoolboy of extraordinary precocity and gawkiness." Barry grew up from being a 'long' baby into a tall thin young man who quickly began developing muscles as his energetic lifestyle had him excavating clay and using his body in construction. School was another matter physically and although Barry is listed in his reports as taking part in athletics, at which he excelled, otherwise he tried to avoid sports.

Takapuna Grammar was a co-educational school run with an iron rod to enforce high standards of discipline and education. Shirley Brickell said she made sure she was home at 3.30pm each day because Barry would come home shaking from school and she would make him a cup of tea and talk to him to calm him down. She feels Barry had a very difficult time growing up because of his unusual nature and she did her best to protect him while he needed shelter.

Both Barry and Romilly have unpleasant memories of their school experiences and recall being absolutely terrified of the teachers. Barry particularly would run afoul the school routine because he was not the slightest bit interested in sport, supposedly New Zealand's national passion, or that whimsical attempt at military imitation then so popular in schools, 'cadets'.

To this day Barry is eternally grateful to his science teacher Ray Scott, who, by turning a blind eye to Barry's activities in the science labs, allowed him to experiment freely with the equipment and chemicals while simultaneously

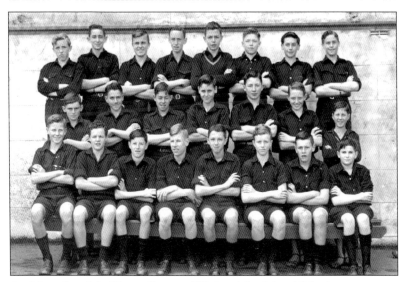

Fourth form class photo, Takapuna Grammar, 1950. Barry is fourth from left, front row.

avoiding sports days and other repugnant compulsory school activities.

Ray Scott explains: "My first recollection of Barry was as a third former at Takapuna Grammar School. He did not stand out in any way until, one day at the end of a science lesson, he remained behind to ask a question. This was a rare occurrence in those days and I, as the science teacher, was all ears.

"'Sir,' said Barry, 'What can you tell me about salt glazes?'

"I have no idea what answer I gave as at that time 'Sir' knew very little about pottery and absolutely nothing about salt glazes. Obviously this was no run-of-the-mill third former; an interesting character, I thought. Some time later I was approached again:

"'Sir,' said Barry, 'I have collected some old bricks from the gasworks. Can you tell me anything about kilns?' Again the student was far better informed than the teacher and all I could do was show interest and encouragement."

Because Barry was intensely interested in practical science, he was soon appointed a 'lab-boy'. Ray Scott recalls: "The lab-boy's job was test-tube washer, reagent bottle replenisher, equipment repairer and general tidier-up. The position was a voluntary one and the work was supposed to be carried out before and after school and during lunch hours. Barry made the chemistry laboratory a second home. Whenever I arrived he seemed to be there carrying out his prescribed duties and sometimes experiments of his own, to which I turned a blind eye. Now Barry was not a natural sportsman, indeed, I suspect he regarded the expenditure of energy unnecessarily as futile. Consequently I would often find him busily at work in the lab during sports periods. I was grateful for the extra work he was doing, he was pleased to be engaged in an alternative activity and in the event of a complaint from a staff member I could always claim the urgency of the job he was doing."

'School cadets' was firmly established at this time and at regular intervals all the boys in the school would parade in uniform under seniors as NCOs and some staff as commissioned officers. During cadet periods Barry could often be found busily at work in the science lab. He thought that falling in and falling out, sloping and ordering arms, marching in step and standing at attention were, like sport, a rather futile way of occupying one's time.

"Later, the student became the teacher when my wife became a potter and was keen to have her own kiln. Barry designed and helped in the construction of our first 'Stonehenge' kiln. I believe he had conceived the idea of dripping old sump oil onto porous bricks in a 'Stonehenge' configuration, setting fire to it with turpentine. The firings often went on all day and all night with the kilns requiring constant attention. To this day I marvel that he, I, and others were able to generate temperatures sufficient to melt earthenware glazes.

"Academically Barry was above average, but his successes both at school and at university were the result of hard and concentrated effort."

Once Barry had equated clay with fire and realised the possibilities of combining the two creatively, he was hooked into pottery. Len Castle had access to a copy of *A Potter's Book* by Bernard Leach and this book was stripped of all useful information, read and reread, challenged and contradicted by the young potters. Early potters' wheels in New Zealand were ones at which you had to stand, not sit and so Leach's design for a wheel at which you could sit was widely copied, built and rebuilt out of scrap materials from the dump. Flywheels could be made from parts of cars, cement-filled tyres and cast-off junk from industry.

Early efforts at the wheel focused on achieving the tallest cylinder you could make without the clay collapsing. Barry used all sorts of techniques to push the clay bodies to their molecular limits.

Hamish Keith remembers: "He could throw clay to a thinness and fineness far beyond its capabilities so the pots had to have a strong base and he made strong-bodied grogged clays. Barry had the most wonderful hands for throwing and if he accidentally put a hole on a pot he'd put a boot on it like a mend on a tyre. He used to take a great interest in those forms which make themselves."

As he got older, Barry began studying the NZR timetables and making excursions on trains around the country. The New Zealand Railway Society formed in 1944 and he joined it in 1955. They organised regular trips with steam locomotives to various spectacular and sometimes little-known tracks. Before the train reached a viaduct, sometimes it would halt and allow those who wanted to, to climb the hill and photograph the train slowly advancing over the bridge. Rarely could Barry be found looking down on the train; instead he would stand under or in the bridge structure, watching how the weight of the train stressed and moved the trusses and bolts. He observed hundreds of bridges, until he could build them in his sleep.

Barry would make innumerable diagrams of his dream trains, rail routes through New Zealand and designs for houses, bridges and kilns. He would visit any gasworks still operating or not yet demolished. He studied the retorts and kilns and the old Victorian machinery which operated year-in and year-out to power the moving parts of the works.

Eventually the time came for Barry to go to university. He left school with good pass marks and a commendation from the principal of the school, Mr Dellow, who said: "I have a good opinion of Barry Brickell, who has an alert and original mind (special hobbies are pottery and music). I regard him as a boy of sound character, high intelligence and pleasant nature."

It was expected in the Brickell family that all their children would go to Auckland University or, alternatively, take some form of training which would fit them for a 'career'. All four children were highly intelligent and talented in various ways. Although it was Barry who began playing the piano it was Andrea who wanted to be a professional musician. Gavin became an inventor and electronics expert and Romilly has had a large and talented family. Maurice, their father, had especially high hopes for them all and perhaps he envisaged a family all working in higher posts in the Public Service arena than he had been able to achieve in the Meteorological Service. Many of Maurice's generation of parents had their promising careers severely disturbed by the Second World War and were anxious for their sons and daughters to have security and lifelong careers.

So it was that Maurice wanted Barry to have security of employment as

Barry Brickell at 22, 1957: envisioning a life of fire, rail and clay.

a result of gaining a sound education. To Barry, this meant conforming to values which were becoming anathema to him. He was caught in a bind. He wanted to honour his father's concerns and with conflicting pressures obligingly forged his way through a university degree. His interests were primarily in rail and clay, not academic study or desk work to create a 'career'.

He remembers that on one occasion Maurice, no doubt desperate yet again to get his message across, said that if Barry worked hard enough he could end up with "a carpet on his office floor". Barry still laughs about this comment, eyeing the bare boards of his pottery.

A 'desk job' was the last thing that Barry wanted for his adult life but after he left school he spent several years working hard, leading a double life as student and potter. He tried out two bursary schemes and worked in the holidays so he could afford to finish his B.Sc. in botany and geology in 1960.

Barry bent over backwards to try to be what his father wanted. He got his degree, worked for the Forest Service and completed his teaching training at Auckland Teachers' College. But all these things simply overlaid Barry's true interests which were in fire, railways and clay.

CHAPTER TWO

DESK JOBS

"For the freeman, a suit and a tie is the ultimate dogcollar of dishonesty."
– Barry Brickell

Barry's teenage years and early twenties, while he finished studying for his degree, were even more filled with extraordinary activities than his childhood. In 1955, his father got him a job working for the New Zealand Forest Service at Tairua State Forest on the Coromandel Peninsula, where he learnt practical silviculture, built very rough wood-fired kilns and made pots from local clays. "But I was interested in the preservation of our natural flora, not destroying it to make way for introduced pinus radiata forests."

The next year Maurice Brickell organised a job in the Auckland Forest Service office so his son could earn some money to keep himself while he attended university. One holiday period Barry accompanied Len Castle and Terry Barrow on a pottery materials hunting expedition to the Nelson area. The early Auckland potters were always hunting for minerals which were not to be had in the Auckland area. They sought feldspar pegmatite for glazes, and clays which could be usefully added to those they had to alter the 'clay body' so it would fire well and make unflawed pots more regularly.

Terry knew a woman, Catherine Philips, who lived in a tiny cottage in the upper Sherry Creek valley, just behind Tadmor, 50 miles south of Nelson. He took their little group to stay with her. Catherine had been single all her life and was in her mid-seventies. She was a natural craftswoman and dyed and spun wool and made woollen garments.

The three men stayed with her one night, greatly enjoying the mountainous views, clear cool air and the cottage which was gently crumbling into the ground. It had a collapsing verandah covered in vines and a garden full of old roses she had cultivated all her life. There was a huge fireplace and coal range. Water was bucketed from the stream nearby. Everything was very simple,

The well-groomed young career man.

homely and restful at Sherry Creek.

Barry and Catherine became friends and corresponded. He visited her again a couple of years later while cycling from Nelson to Westport. She had dinner ready for him and a bottle of her own home-made wine.

When she was 80, Catherine decided to marry an axe-swinging backwoodsman and became Catherine Blowes. She went to live in Nelson, and as Barry was looking for a place to live, she gave him her cottage at Sherry Creek. Barry tried living there for a while but found it was too cold and also too isolated for him to be able to sell his pots easily. It was his first piece of property and subsequently had an interesting history. He could only visit it during his South Island travels and eventually offered the cottage to the British potters Harry and May Davis and their family to live in while they sought residency in New Zealand and a larger home. The Davis family settled in and installed a water pump and kept the place in good order without changing it much. Catherine would periodically visit the cottage and check up on the inhabitants.

Harry and May eventually set up their own pottery in a large house near Nelson and the cottage was again vacant. Some friends of Barry's asked if they could use the cottage and he gave his permission. They shifted in and began clearing the garden and altering the cottage to their liking. Barry was unaware of this until Catherine contacted him and said she was very unhappy with this happening to her cottage which had been her home for so long. When he asked his friends to move out, Mrs Blowes had the cottage demolished.

The combination of the loathsome lifestyle of dressing in smart clothes doing office work he didn't enjoy and trying to study at university resulted in Barry's failing all his examinations in 1956. He resigned from the Forest Service.

He recalls: "I was clearly unsatisfactory for a Forest Service job but both my parents wanted me to continue my education. A lot of my friends were going into teaching and I was persuaded to become a fulltime student on a post-primary teacher's bursary and shared an old cottage with the sculptor John Kingston."

In 1956 Barry applied for a teaching bursary for 1958, since it was too late for him to apply for the following year. He still wished to continue being a student and had to earn some money to keep himself throughout 1957. He looked through the situations vacant advertisements in the *Herald* and saw 'Bricklayer wanted at Kinleith paper mills.' The job was 12 hours, seven days a week shift work and Barry swiftly calculated how much overtime, double and triple time he would make doing this job over Christmas and New Year. He applied for the job and they told him to come down to Kinleith.

Fortunately they never asked him for any trade certification and gave him the job. When he knew he had the job he went to the Auckland Public Library and swotted up on tradesman's bricklaying. He had been building brick kilns for years but this was not the same as the professional bricklaying which was required. He learned brick bonds and cements and bought new tools for the job. To look experienced he had to make the new tools look old, rusty and worn so he wet the tools, hit them and dropped them in mud and cement to give the impression he had owned and used the tools for ages.

At Kinleith, Barry was given a hut to share with another man and for five

STEVE RUMSEY

At Suiter Street, Newmarket: the rent was cheap as the house was becoming derelict.

weeks he lived the life of a shift worker doing very heavy manual labour. He lived on his nerves, had to keep his mouth shut and avoid the union men. An old bricklayer saw his inadequacies and showed him the ropes.

Barry remarks: "How I managed to avoid being sacked as a rank amateur in front of tradesman bricklayers is the best story of deception and cunning of my life. I made £262 in five weeks. That was a lot of money then. It set me up so I could actually go to university and by occasionally selling a few pots I could live. I never expected my parents to pay for me."

As soon as he could, Barry moved out from his parents' home, joined forces with John Kingston and moved into No. 7 Suiter Street beside the huge brewery (now Lion Breweries). The house was very cheap to rent as it was falling down. It leaked everywhere and to deal with this Barry set up ingenious pieces of guttering balanced on bricks and furniture to catch the drips and channel them into pots hanging from the roof. The railway went by past the timber yard next door and was very busy with steam engines puffing in the night. It was heavenly for Barry to be on his own, brewing beer for himself, rather than for his father, listening to the trains racketing by every hour or so, with the good company of John and their other student friends.

Murray Norman remembers his first sight of Barry when he visited John Kingston at Suiter Street. Barry was jumping up and down in an old iron bath

STEVE RUMSEY

Barry with Mormon Pots, Suiter Street.

on the front verandah pugging clay with his bare feet.

It was at this time that the elders of the Mormon Temple in Hamilton commissioned Barry to make seven large urns for their new church. Because he did not have the facilities to pug clay, Barry bought terracotta clay from Crum's brickworks and coiled the first three urns. He arranged and paid for Crum's to fire the pots in their huge salt glaze kilns and sent the finished urns off to Hamilton. A few weeks later Barry received a letter from the elders saying that they did not require any more urns and enclosing a cheque paying for those he had already delivered. He never found out why the commission was cancelled and he still speculates about the reason.

Shirley Brickell would collect both John's and Barry's washing once a week and take it home to wash for them. Many parties were held at Suiter Street in primitive conditions. Deep philosophical discussions happened where the world was verbally made, destroyed and remade a dozen times a night as politics and art vied for importance in their conversations.

Auckland was then so small that, as a student, you could meet Denis Glover, Garth Tapper or Colin McCahon, Rex Fairburn or sometimes Charles Brasch at the parties and Theo Schoon would play his drums and dance Javanese courtly dances as a part of the entertainment.

At an Auckland Summer School in the late 1950s, Colin McCahon and Toss Woollaston were invited to teach painting. All the students and tutors were staying at O'Rorke Hall and had many informal 'yacks and raves'. Barry already knew Colin McCahon but this was the first time he had met Toss Woollaston. Toss invited Barry to stay with Edith and himself in Greymouth any time Barry wanted to visit the West Coast. This was a wonderful opportunity for Barry as the West Coast of the South Island seemed somewhat of an eldorado to him, with the dramatic landscapes, geological formations and the magnificent industrial engineering of the sawmills, steam engines, mines, railways and goldmining archeology of one hundred years before.

So Barry would get on the train and head south, along with his bicycle and maybe a change or two of clothes. He would arrive in Greymouth having travelled for up to four days, occasionally swapping goods trains. Toss and Edith would always make Barry welcome when he arrived unannounced. "They fed me and I'd give them the odd pot. Toss was a Rawleighs salesman then. We would go and sketch and draw, then talk about our drawings. He encouraged me to make my lines more economical and expressive.

"I went railroading alone, travelling about the whole of New Zealand. I was fascinated by the steam locomotive in a bush setting. The refined beauty of railway civil engineering in the landscape, coupled with my love of steam power, took me to remote localities with my camera and sketch pad."

Barry made many sketches during his travels and about 50 were exhibited at the CSA Gallery in Christchurch. Unfortunately a snowstorm filled up the gutters and water dripped down the walls, destroying five of the drawings.

Express train on the old Taonui Viaduct near Ohakune. Barry learned about railway construction by inspecting hundreds of bridges and tunnels on his travels.

He would go on long expeditions investigating old industrial sites and abandoned sawmill railways (bush tramways). He told Peter Tomory that one of his most blissful nights of sleep was spent in the firebox of an old rusty K class locomotive in the railyards at Hamilton. Barry would also explore the NZR timetables for the most interesting routes, taking weekend rides on mixed goods trains, which had a single unheated passenger carriage attached, to Taumarunui and further south, sleeping in caves overnight or in unused carriages on sidings, lighting his primus on the carriage floor and brewing cups of tea for himself, living on railway pies and fish and chips. Returning sated with trains and travelling, with filled sketch pads he would continue his studies at Auckland University.

Barry had never seen himself as a teacher but since Len Castle had been a science master at Mount Albert Grammar School in Auckland and then lectured

PHOTOGRAPH: BOB STOTT

in science at the Teachers' College, it did not seem too horrendous. Teaching was a 'profession' which pottery certainly was not, in the eyes of his parents, so it was worth a try. He wished to please his father who did not hesitate to make it known when Barry's activities were unacceptable.

Elwyn Richardson remembers Barry's stay with him at Oruaiti in Northland while Barry completed his final teaching section at Taipa District High School during three weeks in 1959. Elwyn was teaching at Oruaiti experimental primary school. Barry built kilns for Elwyn at the school and joined in potting with the children, helping pack the kiln, fire it with a salt glazing and then unloading it to reveal all the children's treasures they had made. It was here that Barry learned the stencil techniques he took back to Auckland and tried on his pinch pots. The Oruaiti environment was a magical, creative and stimulating one (detailed in both a book and also a video entitled *In the Early World*, 1960) which must have contrasted strongly with the more disciplined routine of the high school science which Barry was teaching on section.

Elwyn comments: "Barry was never cut out to be a teacher and never wanted to be, but he wanted to make a living. An important factor was that when he lived with his parents there was a lot of tension between the parents about Barry. Maurice Brickell was highly critical of his son and called him a no-good, whereas Shirley, his mother, did nothing but support Barry. Maurice pushed Barry towards traditional success and male stereotypes because he didn't want a son who wanted to be a potter. Maurice wanted Barry to conform and he is an unconforming sort of person. Barry didn't want to offend society yet he doesn't fit in."

Lois McIvor remembers Barry when they attended Colin McCahon's evening painting classes as students.

"Colin had a class in the art school attic and Barry came along. He was an absolute darling of a person. Barry had this thing about trains and viaducts. If you mentioned trains Barry would take out these sheaves of black and white photographs and he'd show them to everybody. He'd taken them while climbing around viaducts, risking his life to take the photos. We thought he was risking his life — we thought he was crazy to do so. We were very careful what we talked about so that we avoided the topic of trains and the sheaf of photos and details about Barry's trains. This was after the painting classes when our class went out to coffee together."

She adds: "He is a very unconventional dresser — no sleeves, sandals. In the city he will have on sandals in the middle of winter, a jersey with the sleeves cut out of it and old pants. I never ever in my whole life have seen him properly dressed up. It's funny the way his mind works — he doesn't conform but would become quite pained that people noticed him. He wanted to be inconspicuous."

Despite his obsessive interest in trains, Barry did have other vehicles in his life. "I had three motorcycles when I was a youth. The first one was a vintage bike I got from a fellow student at varsity. I had a Bown town bike which I got from Terry Barrow and then went to a bigger bike, 350cc which got me here quicker! Now I drive a car into Auckland and back. But I don't enjoy cars — there's no music — there's no aesthetics to me on road transport. It is all in rail. Rail is poetry compared with road. Engineering poetry and practical musical poetry! The flanged steel wheel rolling on a rail is a musical instrument compared to a rubber tyre on a road, which is totally boring."

Barry's life was so filled with rail travel, exploration and potting that it is surprising that he had any time to study for and pass his examinations in botany and geology.

In Auckland in the late 1950s and early 60s Barry Brickell and Dr Denis Hanna, along with many others, built a lot of single chamber updraught kilns with the firebox underneath. Craft pottery as a hobby was proliferating as people went to Avondale College pottery night classes and learned their craft from Patricia Perrin and R.N. Field. Coal was preferred for firing but it was an expensive fuel and the best came from the West Coast of the South Island. Electric or fan-driven oil-burning kilns were other available options for kiln firing. However, a cheaper fuel was readily available.

Denis remembers: "The fuel was the blackest sump oil you could get. This old oil was allowed to stand in drums so the filth could settle to the bottom and the cleanish oil at the top was scooped off to be fed into the kiln. The oil was burnt by being dripped down onto three metal louvres which were preheated by a kerosene fire. These oil-fired kilns belched black smoke and oily smuts which settled on everything but gave quite beautiful glaze effects and I never got these effects any other way. Those kilns only worked well when they made black smoke, a reducing atmosphere — it took eight hours firing flat out. We needed 50 gallons of oil per firing. We got it for free or for a couple of bob from the garage locally. I think that was the beginning of Barry's hands being ingrained with black oil.

"I remember once when we were firing his kiln at Tui Street, Barry took out this red hot firebrick to check how the firing was going and he dropped it on his big toe! As he never wore shoes he had a big wound on his toe. I wanted to take him to the local doctor but he protested. Eventually he was taken and the wound dressed."

Hamish Keith had rented a house at 72 West Street Newton, near the centre of Auckland and in 1960 Barry took lodgings there too. Now Ian McKinnon Drive traverses the spot where 72 West Street once stood. Two tiny pieces of West Street remain and between them is a vast gulf of traffic, motorway flyovers and toitoi bushes planted to deaden the noise and make the motorway seem more environmentally friendly. It is as if the old wooden colonial villas and the lives lived in them never existed. The skyline is festooned with advertising hoardings and trademarks masquerading as the names of buildings. The King's Arms Tavern seems the only remnant of 35 years ago. Denis Hanna recalls:

"It was a rundown house with a very big garden. Barry started building kilns in earnest in the back garden and he quickly became a cult figure. The place was besieged with students, young artists, and crafts people of all descriptions coming to see Barry and gawk at him. He turned out peasant pottery. A lot of beakers for dry red wine. Barry called it his fuel, and he drank huge quantities of raw dry red. I don't know how he drank the stuff! He also made side handle teapots and these were much sought after."

Barry had to make time to study and the Hanna's household in Coronation Road, Epsom, became his refuge. He would bicycle over there and sit with his books in a little back room just off the lounge. Often his botany lecturer Val Chapman would visit and Barry would later imitate Professor Chapman's booming stentorian voice.

Elwyn Richardson comments that at West street, "Barry was making exquisite hand-made pinched chalices and bowls decorated with stencils — Hamish did some but not the best at all."

Hamish Keith comments: "I never wanted to be a potter but you couldn't live with Barry and not be a potter. In 1960 we lived there at West Street for almost a year. We had all sorts of kilns there, a lovely little salt glaze kiln and another upright kiln. We would know it was to temperature because we could cook our dinner on the top. Beautiful pots came out of those little kilns.

"We made a whole series of thumb pinched tea bowls and pinched out great big bowls to try to prove Bernard Leach wrong. His book *A Potter's Book* said nothing larger than a coconut could be pinched and we wanted to prove everything in that book wrong. Lots and lots of pots were made there at West Street. Many were the wet nights that Newton Gully was dowsed with dilute sulphuric acid from our salt glaze firings."

"I was inept at pottery but Barry had all these skills. He was the only person who would go to bed for preference with a board, a cup of tea and a

piece of wet clay, instead of a book, so when I went in and took him a cup of tea in the morning there would be a couple of pots drying on the board beside his bed."

"I decorated some of our pots with stencilled patterns and I made a lot of pots. Barry and I were always mixing up our pots and there are still some which we argue about who made them. We had two or three stamps we used to put on the pots. I used to put a little daisy stamp on

Throwing on the wheel. Tui Street, Devonport, 1957.

mine but we often used any of them on our pots."

Barry has always used the impression of a train wheel as his own personal stamp on his pots, sometimes combined with other stamps but generally alone on the foot of the pot or at the base of the handle.

Hamish continues: "We made storage pots too and there were lovely rich translucent celadon glazes that we used to make. We made our own glazes out of all sorts of strange things. Barry hovers on the cusp of being a sculptor and we had lots of very *big* conversations about what made pots work. We agreed that a clay skin defined the energy of the pot and also that pots were not only objects to be looked at but also used and we had this idea of a tea bowl being the shape for drinking tea. It was the aesthetics of use."

Hamish had recently graduated from art school in Christchurch and he and their group of friends and hangers-on would have long deep philosophical discussions about the nature of 'Art' and related topics. Barry has always felt different from those artists who graduated from art school. He makes his lack of a formal artistic education into either a flaw or virtue, depending upon the situation.

Barry comments that "I have always felt that I entered the studio or 'art' oriented approach to pottery via the back door, rather than through the more customary art school approach.

"The steel-braced arches of the furnaces and the animated puff and clank of the steam locomotive are far more moving than the architecture of our buildings or the streamlined style of our latest status symbols of the transport world; nevertheless I decided to join the Auckland Society of Arts as one of their first exhibiting potters while still a university student. Their exhibition rooms being located in central Auckland on my 'beat' were always a good source of art education and cups of tea and cakes served by the generous hand of one kindly Miss Crisp. Thus I began to pursue with some avidity the nature of art in much the same way as with fire."

The early craft potters had many difficulties to overcome. There was little or no information that was non-technical about how to make glazes and, apart from assiduously looking in your local area for clay deposits, few people knew about studying the geological survey maps for clay types and suitability. The only book available was Bernard Leach's *A Potter's Book*, published in 1940. One copy belonged to R.N. Field who tutored pottery at Avondale College and this book was avidly devoured for any useful information.

Unfortunately Auckland clays were very different from those available in Britain. Basic materials such as fire bricks had to be scrounged from wherever they could be found and luckily there was a resource close at hand. During the early 1960s whole streets of old colonial villas in Newton gully and related areas were being demolished or allowed to run down before demolition to make way for the proposed southern and north-western motorways. These houses supplied the bulk of the bricks and other materials that Barry and some other potters used to make kilns, potting wheels and other basic clay processing equipment. When Jocelyn Fairburn demolished her wash house and coal shed she gave all the bricks to Barry to help build his kiln.

"Those were great days at West Street!" Dr Denis Hanna recalls. "We used to go on expeditions looking for clay. This was before the Nelson clays, which were much superior, came on the market and we had to find our own clay and test it. One of the earliest clays we used was dug from the Takapuna golf course. We would take trains out to Waitakere. We used to explore out there in the dead of night on what we called 'The Looters Train'. We went to the end of the line and we would catch the last train back with bags of clay which we had acquired from the banks there and from the clay works which made sanitary ware. I ruined a couple of my cars filling them full of clay. One very promising bed of clay was at the Mt Eden railway station, a beautiful white plastic clay. It was absolutely disastrous as all the pots exploded in the kiln."

Barry also remembers a clay collecting expedition he did at night in the company of artist Theo Schoon. Both the men had home-made handcarts. Theo walked with his and Barry towed his cart behind his bicycle. He remembers: "Theo Schoon and I had a lot of fun with our handcarts in Auckland city. When Theo took something up it was one hundred percent involvement. He became obsessional about (Hue) gourd growing and he had to have six feet of compost to grow the best gourds. He wasn't a driver so he made a handcart for the city. The cart was made from two old wheelchair wheels and handles and a big box; he'd take the handcart up Karangahape Road and down Grafton Gully and all over but Theo's favourite trip was to the dump. He was always getting the smelliest, dirtiest rubbish for his gourd garden."

Barry and Theo went looking for clay in the dead of night with their handcarts. "Auckland was full of interesting clay. Theo would hear of some clay, perhaps Len Castle would notice the drain diggers digging in the Mt Eden railway yards, Len would tell Theo then Theo would say to me, Let's go down and look at this lovely clay Len has found.

"Theo lived a 24 hour day and it wasn't unusual for him to be awake all night and on this occasion it was probably 2am in the middle of a lovely warm Auckland summer night. I had practically nothing on — it was nice. We went down to the railway yards and filled up my cart with beautiful white clay, covering it with a plastic sheet.

"Theo went home his way and I went home to my flat in Newmarket passing the Mt Eden Jail. Cops were always patrolling the area. I was bound to excite some attention from the police and sure enough a policeman came up to me and demanded to see what was under the sheet in the cart.

"I said 'It's clay'. The policeman said 'That's not clay — there's a body in there.' Well, I was practically collapsing with laughter by this stage. He wanted to know what the clay was for and didn't believe me when I said it was for pottery. He walked all the way home to Newmarket with me from Mt Eden and wasn't very convinced when he saw the dilapidated house I lived in."

Elwyn Richardson remembers those expeditions in the dead of night too: "I never saw him except once do anything morally wrong. Barry, Len Castle and I went out by train to the pottery works. Barry had made several journeys before and he'd take away bricks or lots of grog.

Coiling crocks, Suiter Street, Newmarket, 1958.

PHOTOGRAPHS: STEVE RUMSEY

Sacks of it he would carry away, marvellous stuff it was. Pottery slabs, kiln slabs and all sorts of things were lying about there and on this occasion the caretaker, who lived down the road, appeared and declared he was going to arrest us and Barry, with his gift for charming people, talked us out of trouble."

On occasions Barry, by assuming his educated 'voice' (that of one of his alter-egos Dr Erskine) got himself out of trouble with the law and others.

Barry remembers a very different adventure that is as far from a 'desk job' and as close to his real love as it is possible to get: "Perhaps the greatest day of my student life was venturing for 23 miles on a bush tramway at Ellis & Burnand's steam sawmill at Ongarue in the King Country."

This trip was run by the Railway Enthusiasts' Club in 1957 and Don Black and Merv Smith were also on that excursion train. It set the scene for Barry's eventual plan to construct a magnificent bush railway, imitating the beauty and reversing the use of the original bush tramways which helped strip the native forests of all their timber trees. It was a prelude to Barry's later work saving old locomotives from the scrap heap as a member of the New Zealand Locomotive Preservation Society.

Barry passed his university examinations and teaching diploma by studying hard. He did not find it easy to pass exams. The discipline this required, however, stood him in good stead as he moved into the adult world.

Helen Mason was potting in Wellington and met Barry while he was a student. He was travelling around New Zealand on steam-hauled goods trains during the university holidays when he should have been earning some money. Barry fixed up Helen's first kiln so it would work well, building an upper biscuit chamber onto it. She remembers: "Later, whenever I got into difficulties I would send Barry a rail ticket and after travelling on every goods train in the North Island he would turn up to help me with my kiln."

In his third year at university Barry actually had a favourite route on the railway which took him from Friday until Monday morning to travel and carried him, in trains hauled by steam locomotives, over some of his favourite rail journeys while still giving him enough time in Wellington to look at Helen's kiln and repair it if necessary. He knows this journey and variations so well that he can recall intricate details without hesitation 40 years later.

He recalls: "From Auckland I would catch the Limited Express at 7.15pm on Friday evening, after eating a large Chinese restaurant meal. It would arrive at Taumarunui at midnight and I would fill myself up at the station with rail-

Practices at making classical forms, 1958.

way pies and coffee. Then I would walk up the line to a cave I had discovered in the side of a cutting and spend the rest of the night there, hugely entertained by the steam locomotives passing in the middle of the night, roaring full tilt past my cave going up the grade or drifting down the grade in the other direction. Sometimes a diesel would purr on by as well. There would be anything from four to six trains in the night including the Auckland to Wellington Express which was often hauled by two steam engines coupled together.

"In the morning I would go down at dawn and catch the Saturday morning 6am Okahukura to Stratford 'with car goods' train. It was a train consisting of a locomotive, freight wagons and a passenger carriage which was part guard's van as well. A 'mixed goods' had a separate passenger carriage and guard's van. The passenger carriages were unheated and largely empty. These were slow, slow trains which stopped at every matchbox station to shunt. It was a lovely government attitude in those days which catered for people who didn't have cars and lived in rural areas.

"I loved the Okahukura to Stratford line. It was 85 to 90 miles and took all of eight hours to get to Stratford at 10 to 15 miles an hour, plus shunting at every excuse. It was a 'nowhere to nowhere line' through very rugged country with 26 long tunnels and 30 to 40 bridges. It is an amazing piece of railway construction through papa and sandstone country of great steepness. It is the only link between the King Country and New Plymouth and has never been closed. In the carriage I would set up my 'studio', occupying about four seats near the end of the carriage so I could dive out the door quickly to look at the tunnels and bridges. If I wasn't gazing at these things I would be writing or sketching.

"At Whangamomona there was a major stop, a blow down and re-watering for the steam engine, coal taken on board. I would have lots of cups of tea and pies. Heaps of shunting went on there. The engine would pick up lots of cattle and sheep wagons. If I wanted to catch the 'Picture Train' I wouldn't get to Stratford because at Tahora I would catch the train returning to Taumarunui in order to catch the main trunk Picture Train which was an absolutely unique phenomenon. From 1930 through to the 60s New Zealand Railways timetabled this train on the main trunk line to depart Taumarunui at 3.40pm on a Saturday, a southbound mixed goods train. It went up the spiral in the dusk, a very beautiful experience and got to Ohakune at 7.30pm, giving you time to have a pie and a cup of tea before crossing the road to the Ohakune picture theatre, a classic old building, to watch *Cat On A Hot Tin Roof* or whatever else was on.

"The train stayed in the station until 10.30pm when it was timetabled to depart and went on to Taihape, its destination, arriving at about 3am. I would get off the unheated train covered in all the newspapers I could find. One night an old Maori lady had showed me how to keep warm in a train using newspapers. It was freezing outside and no warmer in the Taihape waiting room where I would bunk down under the newspapers and try to stay vaguely warm until 4.30am when the Express train to Wellington would come in, hissing and clanking, waking me up as it approached the station. This wonderful steam phenomenon came to a halt and I would climb into a warm steam heated carriage and begin to thaw out. I had no money and no ticket. Somehow I negotiated to stay on the train when the guard came around. I would make up imitation tickets and in the dim light the guard couldn't see the difference and would click it and there I was, warm at last and remained aboard until it reached Wellington between 8 and 9am the next morning, Sunday.

"I would phone Helen to tell her I was there and as I was thoroughly dirty I would go to the bathroom at Wellington Railway Station and have a lovely hot bath. Then I would catch the unit out to Johnsonville, walk up to Khandallah to visit Helen and her family and proceed to fix her kiln for her. In the evening she would put me on the steam hauled Limited Express bound for Auckland and I would arrive back in time for my lectures on Monday morning. Of course I was always a write-off on Mondays.

Barry's early decorated, coiled pots based on Sepik River designs, Auckland Museum.

"Occasionally I would miss the Picture Train and go all the way through to Stratford and spend the night in the park which is very nice and has shelters and fast running streams in it. In the morning I would get bacon and eggs or a pie for breakfast. In this way I explored the country from end to end."

Barry was fast moving and anonymous, ragged, tall and thin, had no money and an enormous appetite. Often he would have only enough money for a pie or an apple. Because of his student poverty he would try to make his own fake railway tickets and sometimes they worked, giving him free rides on the goods trains and expresses.

In this way Barry spent his time until he passed his last examination and became a fully fledged degree holding schoolteacher. He was everything his mother and father could have wanted.

It was clear to his parents that Barry was an unusual individual but 'careers' for men were the norm in the 1950s. Maurice Brickell would have been an unusual father indeed if he had not wanted his son to join the nine-to-five workforce and earn a decent wage, marry a good woman and supply a few grandchildren for his father to dote upon. None of these things have eventuated and the Brickell parents have adjusted to the reality of their elder son's individuality gradually.

From 1961 onwards the story is of Barry's choices for himself.

CHAPTER THREE

COLONIAL VERNACULAR ARCHITECTURE 1961-1972

"In vital life we use our environment. To do this needs broadness in concepts, tolerance, human awareness of others and oneself. Awareness of textures, colours, forms and, most important, the spirit or feeling of things. This is how we can extract the very maximum from the minimum of substrate.

This country is big, powerful and exciting. In the raw it is rough, formidable, awe inspiring — absolutely beautiful. Let us have these impressions soak steadily in, making us newer for what we do have. Then, and only then, will we begin to work in a vital way; not checked by strange external conventions that don't belong to us. Let's make pots like basalt blocks or do paintings with the subtlety of the land. Let's be strong and confident in what we are doing. No matter whether it is art, religion or science, be constant and unashamed of your aim or your sin."

– Barry Brickell

Barry moved to an isolated area of the Coromandel Peninsula in 1961 when the roads were all gravel and few public services were available. He was filling a teacher vacancy at Coromandel High School which had been advertised in the Education Gazette and also choosing to live in a place where he had tramped and explored the remote and steep hills with his family and friends. Electricity had recently been supplied as far as Coromandel township. A tortuous narrow gravel road connected Coromandel to Thames. It was more convenient for business to travel to Auckland on the motor vessel *Onewa*.

Barry spent two terms teaching at Coromandel High School but could not face the pressures, withdrawing his services as science teacher at the end of the second term. He found a replacement for the third term so the school was not left with a sudden vacancy.

"I chose my recently graduated friend John Hovell to replace me, much to the chagrin of the Education Department who nevertheless accepted my replacement," he says with a wry chuckle.

Elwyn Richardson recalls: "Barry had trouble in the classroom with discipline. He couldn't understand kids who didn't want to work, who were cheeky. He complained about kids who didn't have his aptitude. He would philosophise and say to the kids, You will never get any knowledge while you carry on like this.

Unfortunately, few children respond to philosophy or the temptations of knowledge when they know the teacher at the front of the class does not have control of the situation.

The student bursary allowance for final year study at Teachers' College was between £5 and £8 a week during the 1950s. A bond system existed which dictated that when you became a qualified teacher this investment in you must be paid back to the Education Department with two or three years' compulsory teaching service. Often this service had to be taken in a remote country area and Coromandel township was one of those places.

Because he was leaving the teaching service within his bond period, Barry

Barry's sketch of the first Driving Creek Railway and Potteries.

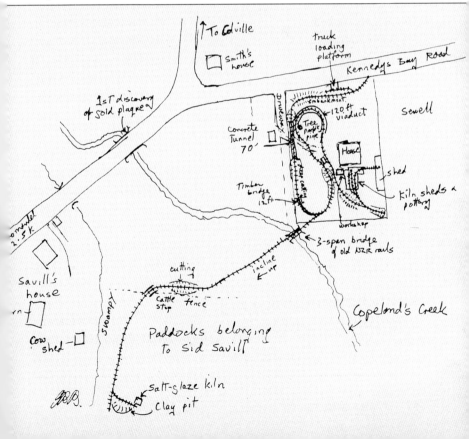

found that he had a debt of £300 to repay to the Education Department. This was a heavy burden for someone who had always been a student. Although they felt keenly for him and wished they could help, his parents had their other three children to feed and educate.

His first home was a rented rambling villa which was soon sold from underneath him. Looking for a new home, Barry discovered that the dilapidated old kauri schoolteacher's house in Top town, at the northern end of Coromandel township, was to let and eventually for sale. Having watched the gradual demolition of Newton Gully for the north-western and southern motorway construction in Auckland, Barry was an enthusiast for what he calls 'colonial vernacular architecture': those old homes built of pit-sawn timber, roofed with corrugated iron. They had a front verandah, hallway with two or four rooms paired opposite each other across the hall and, at the end of the hall, a lean-to kitchen. If you were lucky, someone may have added on a bathroom/laundry and toilet.

Barry wanted this old house and dreamed of restoring it to its former glory as a family home. After slaving and 'potting like hell' for a year he was able to put a deposit on the Driving Creek Road property which was valued at £1100. The house had rotting verandahs and a beehive in the bathroom. It had been crudely 'modernised' at the back with cream and green paint over the kauri ceilings, doors and hall panelling. The kitchen and dining room had been lined with softboard. He immediately began making the house into his own eccentric workplace, a combination workshop, railway, pottery, native plant nursery, gourd garden and home all in one.

Alone in Coromandel, he learned to fend for himself on a non-existent budget. Barry burnt his shoes, tie, neatly pressed trousers and jacket in his new oil-fired kiln. "Freedom at last!" he proclaimed. "I had spent an awful lot of time trying to become something I wasn't. Now I could be as eccentric as I wished, live in shorts and singlets, not worry about my hair or bureaucrats." From then on Barry habitually wore clothes which horrified most mothers, including his own: old oil-soaked trousers, the briefest of shorts trimmed up to an elastic crotch string, cut-off T-shirts, occasionally a cut-off jersey. Some people have even speculated that Barry doesn't feel the cold as he has habitually worn few clothes in all weathers. He assures me he does feel the cold, especially now, but also that he does his best work free to feel the air around his body.

By making the then unusual choice of lifestyle Barry became the second fulltime studio potter in New Zealand earning all his income from sales of his ceramics. Ahead of him was Mirek Smíšek, who began supporting his family selling his ceramics in Nelson in 1956.

"When I started potting my circumstances were very different," Barry recalls. "I had a great natural affinity for clay and fire; pottery and kilns were wonderful for me as a hobby. But when I became a fulltime potter I suddenly found myself on the pottery treadmill. I had to make a living because I had walked out of all the available professions into which my parents had helped me. I had to live off pots: pay for the house, rates, phone, power, food, improvements and afford the railway. One night I woke up in a cold sweat thinking, Oh my God! So many hours a day every day of my life making coffee mugs! Was I really secure? Am I really doing the right thing?

"Mirek was the only one I knew then making a living from pottery and he is one of the people who encouraged me and gave me the confidence I needed."

In 1962 Len Castle also made the same decision and left his job at Auckland Teachers' College to pot fulltime in Titirangi. He too found it difficult to adjust to the wildly varying income that selling pottery brought after having had a secure salary as a teacher.

Peter Tomory, a former director of Auckland City Art Gallery, comments on the financial circumstances of the late 1950s and early 1960s in New Zealand:

"Barry and his generation benefited in enormous measure from the Nordmeyer so-called 'black budget', for it banned all imports except those of general need. This included the banning of all overseas domestic and decorative ceramics. Consequently potters could make a living out of their own domestic output alone. There was only Crown Lynn's commercial output as competition. This provided the craft milieu into which Barry entered and prospered, for crafts people did not encounter the hostility which the painters and sculptors faced in the 1950s."

Despite these advantages, Barry lived on the smell of an oily rag to pay off his debts. He dug clay by hand from parts of local Coromandel roads. On Buffalo Road he improved the ford and on that hillside he cut manuka timber for firewood to sell to the public to make some cash.

"I built myself a boiler and steam engine powered circular saw to cut up the firewood and every time I went to Auckland I would take loads to sell. I even supplied the local fish factory with tea-tree blocks and sawdust for fish smoking. I had the pug mill attached to the steam engine and made terracotta clay. It was fun but I spent as much money setting up my processing system as I made from it."

He made a set of 'star tiles' commissioned for a government building in Rotorua and slaved finding and making suitable clay bodies for potting using the local clays, most of which were not really suited to ceramics as they were largely volcanic in origin. Through experimentation he eventually found a beautiful natural stoneware clay in a local stream bank.

The good Nelson clays were not freely available then for domestic potters' use; indeed few ceramic supplies were available in New Zealand. All glazes had to be made and mixed by hand and tested extensively because they used New Zealand minerals which were different from those in England or Japan which featured in the only reference books to hand. Kiln shelves and any other gear you could not make had to be expensively imported from England. Electric kilns were virtually unavailable and very expensive so oil and wood-burning brick kilns had to be built.

Few potters had such an extensive knowledge of kiln construction as Barry. In addition to building his own kilns, he built many others for schools and potters around New Zealand in the early 1960s, erecting the brickwork and teaching kiln construction for the price of board and food.

Barry's home had no electric power until 1963; although there had been a privately generated supply available locally, his home was not connected to it. He used a wood-fired range, tilly lamps and kerosene stove. He connected the telephone in 1962 and the power in 1963, when he could finally afford it.

In 1962 Bernard Leach, the author of *A Potter's Book*, which had been the only guide for New Zealand's first craft potters, visited New Zealand for a month and Barry went to Auckland to meet him.

"It was with a sense of thrill yet mixed with trepidation that I caught a Thursday afternoon bus to Titirangi, after having made the boat crossing from Coromandel a day or two earlier. At Titirangi I bought a shilling's worth of chips and as it was a fine evening I decided to walk the two miles or so to Len Castle's. I ate the chips in a small bushy cloche by the roadside, thinking that in only 15 minutes I shall be meeting not God, but a man who has led my thoughts since I was 14, 12 years ago."

That week a short film was made of Len Castle and Barry Brickell talking with Bernard Leach and at the end a tribute to him was recorded by Peter

Stitchbury. Barry attended every lecture that Mr Leach gave in Auckland and invited him to visit his Coromandel home. Leach accepted the invitation, much to Barry's surprise, as this was a major departure from the Englishman's schedule. Fortunately he fulfilled Barry's rather high expectations of him. He was a kindly person, much more so than Barry had anticipated for such a famous man.

The visit was arranged with the help of Jane Buckley, a friend of Barry's, and since time was limited, Captain Ladd was hired to fly the little group over to Coromandel for the day in his amphibious aircraft. Barry recalls: "It was utterly different for Bernard Leach. He had never expected anything like Coromandel and he expressed his appreciation for the chance to see such a remote and beautiful place. Jane made us all lunch. I had just finished building my potter's wheel but hadn't even made one pot on it so I asked Bernard if he would like to make a pot and christen it. He made the very first pot on my wheel with his head furiously bobbing around, which was his style. I fired the pot later and kept it for a long time but then it disappeared.

"He was very taken with a small test kiln I had there. It was a very simple, small and efficient drip-feed oil-fired kiln just like those I had been building in Auckland, so by then I had those kilns to a stage of refinement. Bernard Leach never forgot his experience wading out through the mud and pipi shells to reach the plane for the return flight."

Barry had begun thinking about building a railway around his section and decided to call his home Driving Creek Railway. After that he began looking for rails and trucks for his railway track. In mid-1963 Jeff Scholes went to live with Barry to learn potting and art.

"I couldn't get Barry *off* the railway," Jeff remembers. "It has always dominated the larger part of him. He is an incredibly gifted potter as well but his passion for railway to me combines with workaholism. He is addicted to physical work. I have never been so fit in all my life, doing nothing but physical work alongside Barry. To Barry it is abnormal to be inactive. If I was pinching pots Barry would get worried and suggest I went and did some work — he seemed concerned that I would seize up if I sat down for too long. Then it was just the house and the two of us and eventually I needed more privacy. The way to get the most out of this experience was to do everything wholeheartedly his way, which I did. It was like going to a monastery."

Life at the first Driving Creek Railway was intriguing for visitors. It was a

The prototype of Driving Creek Railway, 1968.

joy and a pleasure to call in on Barry Brickell and look at his potting, his railway with the high viaduct, 60 feet of narrow catenary arched tunnel and tight 'Blackberry Bend' where he would speed up to cause unwanted visitors to fall off the railway truck, or would organise Hamish Keith or other friends to ambush the train with a truck load of clay to derail it as one of his 'practical' jokes.

Shortly after calling in and having a cup of tea you would find yourself outside helping Barry make clay, laying bricks, planting native trees in the garden, then an unknown activity; cutting wood, cooking dinner, scraping paint off the wooden panels down the hall because Barry was restoring the house or weeding the railway line. Barry called his villa restoration "a great labour sink into which my friends fell and to which, very often, they never returned."

Peter Hughson, a craftsman from the West Coast, constructed some stairs to replace the manuka pole ladder which gave access to the attic. Jeff Scholes had assisted Barry to build in a pair of opposing dormer windows in the attic and this gave an extra room for guests to stay. Peter Yeates remembers his experiences there in the mid-1960s, the time when he and his friends sailed out of an Auckland party totally unprepared at 2am on a summer morning in a friend's yacht.

"We sailed over the Hauraki Gulf to Coromandel and up the Coromandel River to the bridge, moored the yacht and walked up to Barry's house. It was the middle of summer and he was inundated with visitors so we saw it wasn't convenient to visit. As a result we headed north and in 10 days circumnavigated the tip of the peninsula on foot, a distance of about 110 miles. We didn't even have a tent, and slept in caves and haystacks. It was a very memorable time, a flow of motion. We came back over the Tokatea ridge to Barry's place 10 days later.

"Barry was very welcoming and when he heard where we had been he praised us for our sense of adventure and urged us to stay. At that time he was building a viaduct — a 15-foot high railway bridge — 300 degrees of a circle around a Norfolk pine and out over a slope. He was running his wagons over it; it was quite impressive. He'd gone through about 150 degrees of the circle and we helped him build the other 150. Barry was wonderful with his galvanic influence, in getting people from all walks of life to work for him. He did it in a totally unashamed sort of way. People would ring up and ask if they could come and stay. 'You can come to stay if you are going to work,' Barry would inform them.

"He had a lot of projects going at once. He was integrating all his interests simultaneously — potting, track laying, holistic activities — a petal dance with lots of things happening. Rather like the foraging track of a hedgehog: it is an actinomorphic daisy shape that they make and in a way that is how Barry works. Forging ahead through each day with different things which he does at different times, sometimes potting, or rail laying or building or gardening..."

Barry would sit out on the wide shady verandah at his unique potter's wheel which has no dish or sides to catch drips or spatters. This is because he uses so little water to throw with. I am told the average potter would have great difficulty using this wheel without making a mess but others comment that it is just as good for throwing.

The coiled sculptures would grow and grow, lined up along the shady verandah drying out slowly while Barry would throw two dozen more of those boring coffee mugs to bring in the cash so he could collect more machinery and parts for his railway workshop. In his book *A New Zealand Potter's Dictionary* published by Reed Methuen in 1985, Barry comments about the necessity of making coffee mugs:

Caffeine: The main drug in tea and coffee, which potters seem to need when churning out endless boards of coffee mugs (and other treadmill items of commercial craft-production pottery) in order to either keep up with the insatiable pressing demands of the market or their own local bank manager's persistent requests for a reduction of the overdraft.

Barry was very familiar with both the demands of the public and the bank manager shouting about the overdraft. Like many people Barry preferred to look at his bank balance with half-closed eyes and cope with the crises when he could. If money was available it went into the railway; if not, everyone went hungry until some more pots sold or another commission came in.

Often in the evening he would climb the Norfolk pine and sit on the stump where it had been topped to watch the sunset, sip wine and think. At the foot of the tree his dog Riki-sticks would wait. Riki was an 'important unit' as friend and companion in his busy life. It was in 1962 that Barry had found him as a cold bedraggled puppy under a bush at Reikorangi in the Manawatu. The place where he was found gave him his name. David Black remembers that Riki was "a sheepdog cross-arrangement. Barry had never had a dog and didn't know anything about dogs and because Riki fetched sticks he called him Riki-sticks. He referred to the dog in third person neuter form and when he wanted to tell the dog to stop doing something Barry would say: "It doesn't have to do that" or "Up it gets — down it gets". Riki was an inseparable companion; he was always with Barry."

Riki-sticks eventually became just 'The Sticks', a 'boiler unit' and was fed cod liver oil tablets to prevent corrosion to his 'boiler'. The young potter and his dog were staunch companions from then on. Barry made a special carrier for Riki on his bicycle and carried him everywhere. When it wasn't suitable for Riki to travel with him, Barry would leave him with his mother or another trusted friend to be cared for.

Because of the isolation of Coromandel, Barry had to transport his pots to Auckland to sell them and made frequent trips when he could on the *Onewa* with his bicycle, suitcases full of pots and Riki. Nancy Beck recalls that Barry used to bring his pots up by 'scow'. This was really the *Onewa*, and it would berth at Hobson Wharf.

At times Barry would use the wharf cargo shed as a venue for selling his pots in Auckland. He would phone up the dealers and shop owners who would come down and select what they wanted from the display he arranged on the floor of the cargo shed. He recalls: "One day a harbour board official appeared and told me this was just not on because I was running a commercial business from their premises. I had never thought of this and felt suddenly apologetic and gave the gentleman a pot and he let me continue but this was the last time he would permit me to sell my pots there. I did continue, but more discreetly."

Barry would cart his pots up to New Vision in His Majesty's Arcade. Both of Mrs Beck's daughters worked at New Vision and they remember Barry arriving with his large pots, shadowed by his dog. Barry would then go out and buy two meat pies, sit on the gallery floor, give one pie to his dog and eat one himself. He remembers: "I'd do the rounds of the arty-crafty places, going into these smart galleries to sell my pots and get a small cheque in return." In the late 1960s the *Onewa* ceased making the Auckland/Coromandel voyage and Barry then had to use an old truck to transport his pots to the city.

Peter Tomory gives his opinion about Barry's ceramics in the 1960s. "I always saw Barry as technically a ceramic sculptor or artist, since his approach to the final form of a pot seemed to be inspired more by the need of the clay to be of that particular form than by some established typecast model. He made a one-off mug for me which is so individual in its form that it could be taken for a sculpture, despite its continuing utilitarian function."

It was the 1960s New Zealand style, with flower power spreading the message 'make love, not war' around the world, coupled with the endless strife of the Vietnam war and student protests in the USA on the news every day and on the TV every night. Mini skirts, hot pants, feminism and psychedelic colours were popular. Drugs were being smuggled past a still sleeping customs service. Many of the young people who wished to leave the strictures and expectations of urban society felt Barry Brickell was able to provide an ideal lifestyle for them. He was a potter and from all reports a back-to-naturist, a hippie, an unusual guy who went about mostly naked. Best of all lots of people came and went for free all the time at Driving Creek Railway, considering him to be the guru of New Zealand's first California-style commune. It was set so far out of civilisation they thought it must be hip to live there and soak up the natural 'far out' atmosphere.

Many of these students wanted not to earn a living but to 'drop out' and create a life constructed on non-monetarist principles. Their political stance was that they should simply be allowed to 'be'. It was up to them to define what 'being' meant. Some of those students of the 1960s and 70s are still, in their forties and fifties, wearing long scruffy hair, dealing in drugs and freaking out at their kids who want to have wealth and material possessions.

Like the alternative lifestylers, Barry did not set out specifically to own possessions or wealth but bought his property on Driving Creek Road because that was the most expedient thing to do considering that he loved the house. But there are many ways in which Barry has never been like the 'hippie generation'. He was not into mere existence; he knew what he wanted to do and did it. Mainly he was into hard physical labour and expected everyone else to work as hard as he did. Barry originally began working just with his hands and brute force but as time went by he bought more and more tools and machines to assist in the tasks around Driving Creek and to create the engineering atmosphere with which he likes to complement his artistic side.

Hamish Keith comments: "I have always said Barry is trying to reinvent the industrial revolution without capitalism and without greed. I see Driving Creek Railway as being like an English village out of the eighteenth century. The essence of our discussions when we were adolescents — students of 22 or so — was that you shouldn't have anything around you that you couldn't suffuse with meaning. Since then Barry's been hacking away at the world around him to give it a better form. He's turning exploitation around the other way."

Dennis Hanna observes: "He is an absolute natural with his engineering — bending rails, installing engines — he's absolutely a natural. He'd build potters' wheels by the dozen out of scrap metal. He's no mean artist, too. He used to flog his drawings off at outrageously high prices."

Barry spent a great deal of his time at Driving Creek building his 10½-inch gauge railway. At first it curved around the house from the back to the front, then he laid two sets of points through his studio beside the kilns. In 1963 he devoted most of the year to railway construction and the greater part of the line was built.

The line made its way downhill and to avoid a switchback, Barry built a 350° viaduct which lifted the line up to 15 feet off the ground to keep it on a slight slope down to the milk box, swooping around a loop over the duck pond then threading through the 60 feet of tunnel which was dug as a cutting into the hillside under the driveway and then covered over (see sketch p.43).

Peter Yeates recalls: "Barry's railway was a functional part of his whole world there. A main conversion point was in the middle of his studio where there were two points for different lines; pots were transported to the road on the railway, clay brought in, it was a major working part of the pottery. Barry provided the motive power by setting his bum against the truck. He would lean back against it and start pushing hard with his feet. It was really hard on his body and people would do razor jobs on his feet because he'd grow these huge growths on his heels which would crack deeply and dangerously."

Many people helped Barry construct the original Driving Creek Railway and loved it. They enjoyed being terrified, hunched down to go through the tunnel which had fireboxes in it to give that genuine coal smoke smell and murkiness. The hard physical work was a challenge and Barry was never boring as a companion. There are still remnants of the track remaining in the garden and the tunnel with his inspection shaft beside it still survives underneath the driveway.

Most of all Barry Lett remembers "...his ability to get people to work with him. He was a bit like Tom Sawyer with the wooden fence. You'd be there with the cup of coffee and yak for a while but in a short while you were all outside working. He could manipulate visitors into working for him and you felt a sort of joy at the privilege of working for him.

"Barry would say, Oh I'm so pleased you are here, I need some help with this drum... or moving this clay... it was a joy to participate in his vision and his scheme. The folly or vision or whatever, was the development of the site and the native forest planting. The time that we spent on the railway was much smaller; we were art people and not railway people so we sat around drinking wine after the sun was down. We'd drink a lot of wine at night and talk until the early hours of the morning. Barry would often go to sleep but he'd be up and out before the rest of us. He had Herculean energy.

"Once he asked me to lay a few bricks in the courtyard. 'Feel your way through' were his instructions, so I worked away for a couple of hours and then Barry came back and said 'No! No! Sorry — it's too regular!' and we pulled the bricks all up again and put them in again just anywhere. Sometimes you never knew why. It was as if he was a Zen master who was instructing you in the most roundabout sort of way — 'Oh no it's not organic enough.' No hesitation about offending me or anything, just: 'No. I don't want it that way.'"

Peter Yeates feels similarly: "My view of Barry is that his work has never been fully recognised — or what he really is. People get hold of bits of what he is. He is definitely a teacher with the success he has had in integrating all these earth activities.

"Barry is supremely egocentric. He would sit at the head of the dinner table and go to sleep in the middle of the course then wake suddenly and say 'Ah!' Then he might say something like: 'This place only exists because of my energy!' and we'd mutter 'Go on Barry!', worn out after our hard day's work on his projects.

"He used to talk a lot about 'Zen Castle' as he used to call him. Barry would talk about zen all the time, with a gentle ridicule. This went with the resurgence of the mystical religions. Zen also came through the ceramic world, and he would make soft ridicule about these ideas but would introduce them to people. He is a teacher because his actions would rivet people. He'd succeed purely because he *wasn't* trying to teach anyone. People would see his example and follow it."

Jeff Scholes remembers the excitement and hard work too: "He wanted to share what he was doing. He was so excited about the railway but I found the clay and potting more exciting. Barry was a raw version of all the early potters. To get the clay we would push his handcart about half a mile down the road and lift it over a fence. We would dig the clay out from a stream, put it into sacks and hump it up to the handcart, haul it back and mix a bit of feldspar with it. These days I no longer feel guilty about taking out another bag of ready-made clay but I did for a long time."

All these myriad activities and counter-activities were a part of the magic and the provocation of the Brickell persona, along with his alter-egos or internal companions 'Doctor Erskine' and 'Humphrey P Colefax'. These two people were very much alive and well at Driving Creek and sometimes Barry would use their particular voice tones just to let you know who you were talking with at the time. Occasionally, late at night, Barry would become his railway persona 'Humphrey P Colefax'. He would put on his black felt top hat and shout:

"Time! All aboard!"

Everyone would get on the railway wagon to take the milk bottles down the line to the gate on Driving Creek Road. The truck would run easily downhill swooping through the curves, speeding up through the tunnel and on the way Barry would salute the Len Castle pots set into the cutting, put the milk bottles out and then on the way up everyone would have to get out and push the wagon up the hill by setting their shoulders to the rear end of it and pushing backwards up the hill, stumbling over the wooden sleepers under the rails as they went on up in the pitch darkness of the tunnel and the Coromandel night.

Barry's mother and other friends would always address their correspondence to 'Humphrey P Colefax' care of Coromandel and wonder how the postmistress knew where to send the mail which Barry seemed to receive no matter how it was addressed.

Today Barry is not so often his alter-egos but they are still there underneath. He describes them to me this way:

"It is very difficult to arrange an appointment with Dr, Professor Erskine, he does *not* attend appointments *at all*. It's not easy to know Dr Erskine — he does a vanishing trick.

"Humphrey is quite friendly, he is quite approachable. Mr Humphrey Colefax wears a suit, a coarse tweed suit, is always respectable looking. He is never caught out, never surprised about anything, steady, superficially a very, very agreeable gentleman indeed. He can sound very schemey — have an icy voice on the telephone when you ring him up." (Barry's voice changes to a Dickensian tone.)

"'The name is Colefax, Humphrey Colefax' — he always says that for some funny reason. Especially if somebody wants something... I think he's a puppet of Dr Erskine. It would be inconceivable to have Humphrey in jail, he's too nice a guy, he couldn't possibly be a criminal." Then after some thought Barry recalls: "Dr Erskine has invented a machine which cancels the effect of electricity within a certain radius. You can carry it around in your pocket and anything that depends on electricity stops, gives up, goes out. You would have to be careful how you used it or they would soon know who was doing it, wouldn't they?" He chuckles wickedly to me, musing inwardly about his Doctor Erskine and the machinations of his internal friends.

Michael Draffin and his friends formed a string quartet, sometimes staying at Driving Creek over long weekends to rehearse and occasionally perform for the local people of Coromandel. Barry has always loved chamber music so it was a pleasure for him to have musicians to stay. He will listen to the concert programme until it bores him. He would play cassette tapes of chamber music on tapedecks which became clogged with clay dust, eventually grinding themselves to death. This apparently happens to most potters' tapedecks.

In addition to his home-made instruments for reproducing train noises, he also played the piano as a child and owned a cello for a brief period. Peter Yeates recalls: "Barry is quite interested in sound. He used to play his cello and he'd say 'I have never learned to play it but I like to make animated sounds!' and he'd grimace amazingly while sawing away on it. Amazing collections of notes he'd make on that cello."

Michael Draffin remembers: "It was a bit rough. Barry had no desire to live with care and elegance. In fact it was dirty and grotty — I'm a bit of a fusspot I suppose. We knew there would not be gourmet food at Barry's. So Stormy Lane and I took down a great big pot of curry and ate that. When we got up in the morning there was a pan of sausages left on the bench and the mice had been at them. I said to Stormy, Well we can't eat those damn things, the mice have been at them. Then Barry came in and said, 'It looks as though the old mice have been having a go at it' and picked up a sausage and put it in his mouth!"

Barry has never been one to waste food. Somehow he has survived on whatever anyone else wanted to cook in the kitchen. If he was lucky Yvonne Rust would be visiting and insisting upon doing all the cooking. His own cooking will stretch to mashed potato with onions, poached eggs or sausages. Food is fuel for physical work, not created for its own sake as an artistic experience like music or painting.

Yvonne Rust and Barry Brickell have had a close, sometimes competitive but fruitful association ever since they met in 1960. She recalls: "I knew of Barry Brickell but hadn't met him. One week he suddenly popped up in Christchurch and my students (Warren Tippet and Michael Trumic) surprised me by inviting him around in the evening. They used all sorts of excuses to keep me there at home, when I would have gone to the studio, until Barry arrived.

"He was dressed in his ill-fitting awkward trousers that didn't meet up with his body and hung from him loosely, touching his body occasionally. These were his formal pants for train travel. He would cut off the sleeves and logos from his shirts so they wouldn't look so formal. He had sandals on, very brief ones, mostly bare feet and at night he would put his feet up on the table and put butter in the cracks in the skin on his feet. Groups of us would have emotional 'raves' where the house quivered with the voices vying with one another. These were no ordinary discussions but 'raves' about all subjects, not just pottery."

Barry's capacity for food is legendary and he will eat all that is left over from a meal to fuel his body for the next day of incredibly energetic hard work. Yvonne Rust recalls one occasion when Barry visited her in Christchurch in 1962. She threw a party for Barry; 22 people were invited and Yvonne, as is her habit, cooked a lavish meal of roasts, Hungarian goulash, baked potatoes, salads and fruit crumbles for them all. They waited and waited but only six of the original invitees turned up to meet Barry so he sat at the table and ate all the 14 missing persons' dinners as well as his own. "And I don't skimp on food either," says Yvonne, laughing at the memory.

It was this eccentric atmosphere at Driving Creek Railway, which vaguely resembled but essentially was not the 'tune in, drop out' mentality of the hippie era, to which hopeful young men and women would come. In ones and twos, sometimes large groups. Some staying for years, some for only a day or two.

It was confusing for them; looking at Barry they couldn't figure it out. Why was he so charismatic and yet refused to teach or lead them? He didn't smoke or take drugs. He was totally innocent of all guile with women and men. Who is he? What is he?

Generally, if they were not working with Barry, visitors were smoking, drinking, playing music, getting stoned and lounging around in the sunlight and warm evenings of Coromandel while Barry worked continuously. A dynamo of energy, stumbling over them, setting them to work when he could get them to work, buying food if he could afford it, desperately repelling the amorous advances of those young women who would get it into their heads that he was an 'eligible bachelor' whose children they wanted to conceive, or worse, to marry and reform him. Dress him in shirts with sleeves, walk shorts, a paisley tie, socks and shoes. A fate much worse than death to Barry!

Many of Barry's friends dating from the 1950s have commented that they avoided Driving Creek Potteries during those years when the hippies were there. They make scathing remarks about the poor quality of people Barry allowed to settle around him at times and wonder how he put up with them. Some he did not put up with and threw them out. Some became good potters and some did not. These were anxious times for Barry and his faith in humanity was strained.

Often a visit from friends would fizzle out because he wasn't at home but 10 other people were settled in, seemingly forever. Sometimes Barry was escaping, sometimes he was away travelling by rail for the love of it, or rescuing a steam engine in the King Country or was on his way to the West Coast to visit Toss Woollaston or Yvonne Rust.

Barry would visit the Ikon Gallery in Symonds Street every time he went to Auckland to deliver pots. It was there at the end of 1963 that he met Michael Illingworth, a painter who had just arrived from England and was destitute. Barry describes him as having a spaniel-like long sad face. Michael wanted to earn some money so Barry offered him a job cleaning bricks for kiln building. Barry was unaware that Michael had a drug problem and expected him to work hard cleaning bricks. Barry also gave him a room at the front of the house in which to paint.

For several months Michael lived with Barry and would follow him around, talking constantly in a plaintive voice about the various ills of western civilisation. Barry recalls: "Michael was a great painter but he had a face like a cliff and evoked in me a powerful mood of depression around the house. He was scathingly critical of other painters. He had no energy and he didn't realise how he was irritating me, talking so negatively all the time. He told me all about sex, which seemed to preoccupy him and it was the last thing I wanted to know about. I just couldn't communicate with him. He would moan occasionally at night and leave the lights on all night in his room."

Eventually Maurice Brickell got to hear of this Michael Illingworth and drove down and evicted Michael from the house after a huge argument. Barry did not want to be involved in all this strife and was in fact rather relieved when Michael returned to Auckland.

In 1965, coinciding with the Arts Festival in Christchurch, the great Japanese folk potter Shoji Hamada was invited as a guest artist and he chose Yvonne Rust's studio in which to make his pots for the two weeks he was in New Zealand. Extolled by Bernard Leach, Hamada was the 'God' of style, ancient Asian technique and culture for many of the craft potters of New Zealand.

Yvonne recalls: "Barry was pretty arrogant when he came to see Hamada in March 1965. Some of the men were acting like young guns and they didn't think Hamada was going to teach them much but they were eventually humbled before the energy of Hamada.

"The women had done all the setting up for Hamada in Christchurch but the moment Hamada arrived all the young guns became his right hand men. He was such an incredible potter that he only got his fingers covered in clay up to the second knuckle and never got any clay on his spotless black robes.

"Hamada would have a siesta in the middle of the day at the studio and the day I was there on guard in the other part of my studio I heard Hamada come out. He had picked up one of Barry's pinch pots and was grinning. He really looked at it and had a grin. It was a private moment and I didn't interrupt him or ask him about it. Later on Hamada bought only one pot and that was Barry's, which I thought was an insult to Hamada — lots of people had given him pots of their own. 'Why didn't you give it to him?' I asked Barry.

"'No, no... no no no...' said Barry in that way he has. Hamada explained to me that New Zealand was a primitive place with no artistic qualities about it — a peasant land and that Barry's pots portrayed the spirit of New Zealand very well."

Few people realise that Barry is a painter as well as sculptural potter. Lois McIvor says this: "Barry loves painting. He's a great fan of painting and has a wonderful visual sense. He could have been a good painter. He's had a tremendous influence on New Zealand pottery and was one of the first to get into the sculptural pottery. The big pots with the *big* spaces are so much more difficult to do, very hard to fire. I think he was really one of the first people to do this. Barry never used brightly coloured glazes — he was a man always very close to the earth — has a New Zealandness."

Concurrently with building up his reputation as a great studio potter, Barry was still exploring railway history and enjoying the last of our steam locomotives before they disappeared forever.

In 1966, nine years after his original trip on the Ongarue tramway, Barry took David Black with him back to Ongarue. David was a young man of only 18, but full of enthusiasm for King Country sawmills, bush tramways, steam engines and engineering of all kinds. David continues the story:

"I soon got to know Barry and we found that we had a kindred interest in the bush tramways of the King Country. At the time that area was in the immediate post-milling days and there was a lot of sawmill equipment still lying around. Barry had a Fiat 600 and I met him at Mananui, south of Taumarunui, where we found two bush tramway steam locomotives in a shed at Ellis & Burnand's old mill site. The engines were in a shed and still in good condition. Then we drove on to Taringamotu where there was still an operational tramway and a sawmill team. We drove on to Ongarue. Here was the sawmill, largely dismantled, but there were signs of the tramway and one steam engine was still there.

"Next we drove on to Mangapehi which was uncharted territory to us. We knew all about the tramways that were connected to the main trunk line because we always travelled via train. But this remote road travelling was even more rewarding. We saw the smoke stack of the Mareroa sawmill in the distance as we drove towards it and there we found a completely intact mill town, mill houses, and a steam mill still simmering hot in the evening. There was also a beautiful Tangye steam engine still intact. No one was around at the mill and we were directed to the local club which appeared to be a shed just out of town. Once we got there we just couldn't buy beer for ourselves because all the mill workers wanted to buy us a beer, they were so pleased to see someone still interested in a steam sawmill.

"We got a huge amount of 'loot' from that trip. Ellis & Burnand's first sawmill was at Otorohanga and their intention at Mananui was to barge the timber down the Wanganui River. This wasn't feasible and so they waited for the main trunk line to come through, which it did in 1908. Ellis & Burnand built the main tramway called the Pungapunga tramway and we found their

The first train rescue: Richard Stratford and Barry Brickell changing axles, Mananui, 1966.

abandoned office at Mananui complete with various records and survey maps. Barry was really very interested in these survey maps because he wanted to see how the original surveyors did the surveying of the tramways."

This excursion later led to more trips through the bush and along virtually impassable roads to discover the bush sawmill and tramway remnants abandoned in the remote places of New Zealand. The eventual formation of the New Zealand Rail Preservation Society in 1966 was a result of these explorations.

David continues: "Because of this interest we had in the bush tramways, Barry, myself, Merv Smith, Tim Hunter, Richard Stratford and Kerry Bennet decided we would form a society, The NZ Rail Preservation Society Incorporated (NZRPS). We wanted to preserve all the old steam engines and save them from scrapping. I was 18 years old and became the first president."

"By negotiating we managed to get those two bush tramway engines left at Mananui given to us by Fletchers who had ended up owning the mill site. They were an old Price 'C' and a Price 'CB' class, engines which had been built in Thames. We didn't know what we were going to do with these engines but as a temporary measure it was possible to move the engines up to Taringamotu where there was still a tramway and store them there. We could do this because the tramway had used the same gauge as the main New Zealand Railways (NZR) rail system.

"So we hired a DA diesel locomotive from NZR and arranged to have a 'special' train scheduled. Then Barry, myself and Richard Stratford went down and repaired the engines before they could be moved. The axles had very sharp wheel flanges because the engines had done so much yard work and the railways inspector said that we had to change the axles for some new ones with blunt wheel flanges as without proper shaped wheel flanges they would not be permitted on the main trunk line because the line would be damaged.

"So we cast about for some spare axles and found some way down south lying around somewhere between Ohakune and Taihape where another engine had been wrecked in a farmer's paddock. I went to get the wheels and axles (which are all in one piece) and we jacked up the two engines and fitted the new wheels and axles. It was an enormous job — a lot of engineering involving at least a week's work for all of us to repair the engines so they would move.

"Then in order to couple the two engines together we borrowed an NZR 'WAb bar' which fitted between the engine couplings and tied the two engines securely together. This made up the 'train', composed of the DA diesel loco-motive (hired), the two engines (C and CB) coupled with a WAb bar and a guard's van coupled to the rear to make up a real train following the regulations then which decreed that a guard's van was compulsory on all trains.

"The next massive problem was moving out onto the main trunk line as the local council had sealed over the rails that crossed the main road. Barry rode in the front cab and I rode in the rear cab and very, very slowly we towed the engines across the seal and over the Wanganui River bridge and up to Taumarunui. A properly authorised private rescue train.

"Barry and I decided that the train, being a scheduled train, would stop at Taumarunui station and we would have a railway pie. After we all had a pie and a cup of tea the journey continued on very slowly to Taringamotu and there we took the train off the main trunk line and were met by the mill manager.

"The mill's own petrol-driven locomotive towed the engines up the tramway line but Barry was very worried about the crown wheels jamming in the clay so he went on ahead of the train with a spade, digging a groove up ahead of the engine where the crown wheels would otherwise dig into the mud between the rails. It wasn't really necessary but Barry was concerned so he kept on digging. Up past the Taringamotu mill the line had gone on into the bush

The Mananui train rescue: they decided to stop at Taumarunui for a railway pie and a cup of tea.

another 15 miles and a short section remained but it was now all under mud — up to three feet deep — so we had to dig this line out by hand in order to store the engines there.

"NZRPS commandeered two of the single men's forestry huts, Barry equipped them with pottery and we worked on those two engines there at Taringamotu for some time as we fully intended to preserve them. Barry was less involved during the preservation work on the engines but finally it was he who went down and boarded the engines up, locking them to protect them from vandals."

The engines sat there until 1971 when the mill closed and NZRPS were told they must be moved. There was no shortage of takers for them. The CB engine went to MOTAT and then went with the Bush Tramway Club to Pukemiro Junction to be restored by Richard Stratford. The C engine went to the Tokomaru Steam Museum near Palmerston North.

During the decade of the 1960s Barry and Yvonne Rust visited each other frequently, making the trip between Christchurch and Coromandel or Greymouth at least twice a year. Barry loved exploring the West Coast, travelling mostly by train and finding old steam engines of all sorts where they had been abandoned in the bush. Steam lasted much longer on the West Coast than anywhere else in New Zealand so the region was a treasure trove of old

DAVID BLACK

machinery which Barry plundered for parts and scrap for his own engineering.

Yvonne was exploring too, after she moved to Greymouth in 1966, looking for clays and other resources in order to set up her own pottery and school, succeeding the one she had created in Christchurch. They had discovered the abandoned site of Stewart's Brewery separately and compared notes on its suitability as a pottery. When Yvonne had finally negotiated a lease of the large building Barry joined her to help turn it into a pottery.

She recalls: "After much struggle I managed to rent the old Stewart's Brewery just out of Greymouth. Barry was on his way down and said he was getting off the train in Greymouth at 6am and would meet me there. So we met at seven in the morning and I cooked him paua patties because he loved them.

"We stood in the top corner of the brewery and looked down through it, this dilapidated building of two 30-foot square rooms. One was higher than the other by 15 feet. There were huge pipes winding around inside it that people had vandalised, tanks, big chunks of concrete — it looked like total chaos that day while we were having breakfast. I left Barry there and went off to teach from 9am to 3.30pm. When I came back from teaching Barry had taken down all the pipes that had filled the huge room using an enormous railway crescent to unscrew them which he had just acquired from somewhere. You never ask Barry where he acquired things from. He took a delight in unscrewing these huge things using this new tool he had just found.

"This was about February 1966 and in May he came back and built the huge round coal-fired kiln I had at the brewery. Barry arrived in the May holidays and declared that he was going to build me a kiln out of the bricks I had collected. Away he went taking it all out of my hands and built a beautiful round coal-fired kiln. I was only allowed to be hard labour in the building. He built a round kiln because the bricks were sloped on one side since they had come from the waste brick pile at the Brunner coke ovens which Barry and I had rediscovered. Stewart's had been a one-man brewery and the old owner died on the day I had my first firing — that was the firing that Barry did. He fired it once to show me how and then left so I had to fire it from then on, having only been shown once.

"While I was teaching he would be at the brewery with my pottery students and they benefited from that. He lived there while I lived at the student hostel and Barry changed the brewery around to how he liked it because he tended to live there all day and night.

"He kept popping up at different times in different areas and we would do something exciting like look at trains or go into the bush and cut loose a steam engine from the forest. He used the West Coast to get a lot of his railway lines and machinery."

Barry tried to regenerate the weka in the Coromandel, by catching them on the West Coast and taking them home with him. He had obtained permission from the Wildlife Service to do this. Weka were plentiful in the South Island and Barry recounts one episode with them out in the bush on a rescue mission dismantling an old bush loco at Bell Hill, near Greymouth.

"It was a Johnson A locomotive and was made in Invercargill by Johnson Brothers engineering works. David wanted to save it as it was the last of its kind in the whole country. One day I was busy cutting the steel cabin off the frames; I stopped for lunch, got out my primus and frying pan and cooked a couple of bangers (sausages). Then I continued cutting while they cooked and out of the corner of my eye I saw a weka approach the frying pan. I thought, he is *not* going to grab a sausage — they are hot! But blow me down if he didn't put his beak in and hooked out a banger!

"So I said to Riki-sticks, Do something about it! After it! He gave a woof and got up and began to do something about the matter. The weka had scuttled off and by the time Riki got to it the weka had dropped the sausage which I put back into the frying pan. After that I posted Riki by the frying pan to guard it from the weka so he had to have a sausage too."

A lot of weka would venture into the brewery, seemingly very tame until you shut the doors when they would go wild and always find some way of getting out again — it was just too hard to catch them. When Barry finally introduced some weka to Coromandel they seemed to die out quite soon, or perhaps were killed by the cats and dogs that live in the bush and on the farms. There are still no weka stealing food at Driving Creek.

A number of the potters at Driving Creek spent time learning pottery skills with Yvonne, both in Christchurch and then for seven years in Greymouth where she taught art classes at the high school and ran her pottery school at the brewery. There she taught her pottery students her own philosophy of hard work, producing enough pots to fire the big circular coal-fired kiln weekly, a tremendous feat.

As soon as he could afford it, Barry employed Roy Cowan and Hansen's Engineering to build him a 10-inch gauge engine with an Austin Seven motor.

It was planned in 1966, built and completed in 1967 and on it were two brass engine number plates, 'DCR 167', cast by Greer Twiss. The plates sat proudly on the sides as the locomotive pulled the four wagons Barry had in his rolling stock. It was Barry's first locomotive and he was intensely proud of it. Certainly it made a great change after all the years he and others had spent pushing the wagons up and along the line. There were one or two people Barry regarded as having their 'ticket' to drive DCR 167. Their competence was assessed by the manager of Driving Creek Railway, Humphrey Colefax.

In 1968 David Black needed a home and lived at Driving Creek for about eight months. Then the spelling of Mr Colefax's name had not yet been firmly established, David remembers. "We had many discussions about the spelling of Colefax over a dry red. Sometimes it was Humphrey P (Ferdinand spelt with a Ph) Köhlphacks; 'Humphrey' because he said 'humph!' when presented with a problem, or 'Coalfacts' as spelt by steam engineering men who deal only in facts. Barry loved to observe people with various interesting personalities and Charles Brasch interested Barry intensely because Charles used to come to visit and was completely bewildered by everything about Barry. He used to say 'Really... really... ?' about everything."

Barry, of course, would imitate him.

David continues: "Barry made me extraordinarily welcome as he realised that I had come to a bit of a crossroads. I had thrown away a career and he provided me with a home. When I first went to Driving Creek, Barry was drilling holes in rails with a hand drill and cutting rails with a cold chisel or a hacksaw and I said to him:

"Do you want to build a railway or do you just want to drill holes? Barry was pretty Presbyterian about this and initially resisted the introduction of technology. But eventually I was given the authority by Barry to go and spend some of his money. He gave me a Kauri tobacco tin full of money and I bought him some gas cutting equipment and a Young's model C arc welder, all brand new. I also bought him a large Wolf electric drill."

Barry reminds me that he spent several years paying this investment off at the bank. Then he got enthusiastic about moving towards machine tools and turned his attitude around quite rapidly. He employed the neighbour next door to build him a workshop to house the tools and in the workshop Barry installed a metal lathe.

Sid Savill, the farmer next door, allowed Barry to extend the railway onto his property. So Barry and David built a new viaduct across the creek into Savill's property with inverted NZR 90lb rails as main bearers and sat the rails on the webs. They spanned the creek with this bridge and it was a very competently constructed viaduct. Then Barry finished the planned railway which extended to a small lake and at the end of the line he built a new salt glaze, coal-fired kiln. Barry created in total about three-quarters of a mile of railway track on a section of just over an acre including the 'borrowed' section of line which went across the stream into Sid's property.

David comments: "Intuitively Barry is very skilled and he also understands first principles. Barry has spent his whole life observing structures and always looks at every bridge so now, thinking about how to build a new structure is quite intuitive."

In 1969 Barry lived for some months on the West Coast (which has some of the best clays in New Zealand) having a working holiday with the other potters and crafts people there. David Black, Yvonne Rust and Peter Hughson were all living on 'the Coast' at the time, along with other old acquaintances. Everywhere Barry went he knew someone he could stay with, have a bed for the night, a few glasses of dry red and a good 'rave' about art or pottery or the state of the world. There Barry collected lots of 'loot' to take home in his old truck which he drove very carefully, due to his short sightedness for which he has never worn any spectacles. Yvonne claims that whenever she was with him, Barry would let her drive so he could watch the scenery easily.

Rod Buchanan, a beekeeper from Greymouth, wanted a replacement boiler so David and Barry found a steam winch north of Karamea which had just finished operating. The boiler was still in good condition, and the owner gave it to them to take away. Barry and David went to get the boiler.

David continues: "We took off for Westport in an old Bedford truck which belonged to Rod and stayed the night in the old Seddonville pub. We drove the truck for miles up mud roads into the middle of nowhere and found the Dispatch 14.9 hp underfired multi-tubular winch boiler. (They made them 14.9 hp because over 15 hp the operator needed a second class steam ticket.)

"We had a lot of tools on the truck, we always took a lot of gear and we used timber jacks a lot. There wasn't anything you couldn't do with these jacks coupled with an oxyacetylene set. It was raining all the time. On the West Coast you never stop working in the rain, you just pull your hat down further, wear a 'Lammie', turn your pipe upside down and occasionally look up and say 'Fuck the rain!' We blew off the bolts that held the boiler to the chassis and then the problem was to get the boiler up onto the truck. We pondered this for a while and noticed that nearby there was a small bulldozer, an Alice Chalmers HD11.

"With this we dug a hole beside the boiler big enough to fit the whole truck and pulled the truck into the hole with the bulldozer. This got the tray level with the boiler then we slid it over with jacks packing it up with 4x2 inch timber runners and tipped it with a huge crash onto its side on the truck — it was square because it had the firebox too. We then had to get the truck out of the hole and to do this we had to dig a ramp in the mud in front of the truck and bury the bulldozer in another hole to winch out the truck. We jacked up the back of the truck and spent hours getting it out of the hole.

"This took us the whole day to achieve and when we got back to the pub we were filthy, thirsty and hungry as hell looking forward to a hot meal and a bath. During dinner at the pub we realised that the truck was overloaded to hell, and so, to avoid the Ministry of Transport, we took off that night and got to Greymouth at 1am, dog tired. It was a very heavy load for that truck, making it difficult to drive.

"We got to Rod's and turned into the driveway but just there the truck bogged down on the main road 100 metres from the final position for the boiler. It was still raining so at 6am we went down the road, got a bulldozer, pulled the truck out and up the hill, jacked the boiler up and slid it down a wooden ramp onto the ground, where it landed up the right way and there it has sat ever since.

"Then there was the interesting exercise of repairing it and Barry was very interested in this operation. We cut a lot of the tubes out of it and re-tubed it and that was when we got to know the Marine Department inspector, a timid man called Mr White. He tended to say no to everything because he never seemed sure what he should say yes about.

"Anything that looked a bit dodgy we never showed Mr White. Barry was quite fascinated by the whole process of restoring the boiler. He made up a tube plate out of clay incorporating all the faults and cracks that would make a Marine Department inspector tear his hair out. Then we had a 'steaming up' party. We had done a hydraulic test on the boiler and decided it was in good condition but the steaming up party was still illegal. We invited the Marine Department inspector to the party, but he didn't show.

"We fired the boiler up and had a full head of steam in the early evening. As well as two engines we had connected an American chime locomotive whistle to the boiler and started blowing it as the party progressed. The elderly residents of Greymouth associated this sound with a ship in distress on the bar so lots of people rushed down to the wharf looking for a stranded ship."

While on the West Coast Barry found a traction engine boiler which he bought for $10. It too required hauling out of the bush with a bulldozer and Barry then had it transported to the Manukau Harbour on a ship and eventually delivered to Driving Creek where he began to restore it. When he moved to the new Driving Creek Potteries he sold it to Bob Mann as he had no further need of the boiler.

Eventually Barry returned home to Coromandel with his truck laden with paintings, machinery, tools and pottery. The original ceramic boiler plate still sits at DCR and few people realise the series of visual ironic jokes inherent in the design, which represents the opposite of a new boiler plate.

In 1970 he bought a launch called the *St Lawrence*. He had become interested in boats again since the railway was almost finished. The *St Lawrence* had been used as an officer transport in the 1900s. It had a badly damaged Fordson four cylinder diesel engine. Barry wanted to visit Yvonne Rust that Christmas. So he, David Black and Richard Stratford lifted the old engine out of the boat. David recalls: "We spent days overhauling this boat engine. It had everything wrong with it and then we ran out of time. We literally went down, bolted the engine into the boat and took off for Auckland with Richard and I between us keeping the engine going. We got to Auckland and Richard crewed for the rest of the voyage as an engineer although he was not as experienced as I was." David left them to join his family for Christmas. Yvonne continues:

"Barry had bought himself a launch and said he'd take me from Auckland to my Parua Bay property in Whangarei Harbour. We did this twice on two different boats. This trip was hair-raising because we hit the beginning of Cyclone Rosie. Bad weather kept hovering around – it was absolutely terrifying.

"Barry wasn't familiar with the engine because he had just bought the *St Lawrence*, so he wanted to check the engine. We were fighting the waves and he left it to me to steer the boat. The others on the boat were sick as anything so it was up to us. I held the tiller for two hours while he went below and adjusted the engine and after those two hours I was exhausted, but Barry had held the tiller in that weather for seven hours already!"

David continues: "They hit very bad weather. It was Cyclone Rosie, and I was very worried, going over every nut and bolt of that engine in my mind because I knew that if that engine stopped they were in real trouble with the extremely bad weather. It's the way you think as a young man — his life depends on that engine and he's alright because I fixed it and did it right."

Eventually the *St Lawrence* reached Parua Bay and Richard was rushed to hospital seriously ill with Hepatitis A. Barry also remembers that he spent a lot of time trying to keep the *St Lawrence* afloat because it was full of leaks and gradually rotting away. Barry and David were close friends for many years, working together on many other engineering and railway projects. Barry was best man at David and Christine Black's wedding in 1971.

"One of the most memorable things was when Barry sailed the *St Lawrence* to Auckland for our wedding and he parked 'The Sticks' outside the church for the wedding. When Christine came down the aisle on her father's arm the Rikisticks followed them down the aisle and he sat behind us on the carpet while we were married. This was in a posh Remuera Church. Barry wore jeans and a jersey which is what we expected. After the wedding reception we took the *St Lawrence* with Eric Hood and Richard Stratford and motored up the Albany Creek, stopping at Beach Haven to get fish and chips for tea. That was perfect for our wedding day."

David adds: "Barry has this incredible joie de vivre that comes from his family and the art that comes out is the outpouring of the joy within him. He can look at the mundane and see incredible things in it."

Barry looked at the isolation of Coromandel and made his own world there. He became a source of inspiration to many others who came to see, stay and eventually, learn.

The first Driving Creek Railway was an holistic achievement with Barry centred in it. The steel tracks of the railway united everything with shiny parallel steel lines which traversed the property, leading you from one activity to the next. Driving Creek became a place which had thousands of hours invested in it but was based on ideas which had nothing to do with making money. Would Barry spend the rest of his life on this property? Already his eye was roaming, looking for a bigger project more fitting for his talents.

(Right) How do you separate the artist from his work? Barry at Driving Creek, 1969.

PHOTOGRAPH: STEVE RUMSEY

CHAPTER FOUR

THE PSEUDO GURU
1973-1979

"I am a visionary individual and have my own thoughts. I do not want to be conditioned in my outlook by conventional or popular opinion and am prepared to be labelled an eccentric if necessary. I cannot teach: I am far too busy with my own work. People educate themselves when they are fulfilled and happy in their work. There is no such thing as teaching, only learning."

– Barry Brickell

The first Driving Creek Railway had become too small for Barry's vision for himself and he sought something larger to occupy his stupendous energy.

Barry remembers: "When I was at the first Driving Creek Railway it was on an acre and a bit and within a few years I was ready to burst out; it was becoming too small for me. I felt hemmed in. The neighbours complained about the smoke from the kilns and so I took the world in my arms and bought 500 acres of scrub land for £1000 at Waikawau, an hour's drive north of Coromandel township. I built a bivouac group of huts on a ridge and escaped there for the summer holidays, enjoyed the landscape there, did some writing, walking, tree planting, thinking and beachcombing.

"I had grand schemes and dreams for a railway across the peninsula. I was going to sell Driving Creek, move up there and build a magnificent mountain railway system. Move there with all my kilns. Then I realised I had to drive there and drive back and there was just so much driving involved, because it is a remote place, that I would have to buy a van and transport would always be a hassle and I realised I wanted to be more in touch with my city friends.

"Some local people branded me as one of the first hippies, not that I ever led a hippie lifestyle, but I did my own thing in my own way and some elements of my outlook belonged to the hippie world which was then on its way, so people confused me with a hippie.

"I always had my eye on my present property which was then unavailable for purchase. The owners didn't really use the land and in 1973 they decided to sell it. I thought well, this place is perfect because it is close to Coromandel town, within bicycle distance and I can get my supplies easily. Not too far to shift all my Brickellbrac from the first DCR which is just down Driving Creek Road.

"I managed to sell both of my properties to raise the money to buy this piece of land. I said to Tom and Wailin Elliott, I want to buy this piece of land, the price is $8000, will you give me $8000 cash for my house on Driving Creek Road? They said, Yes, not a problem.

"So I bought these 60 acres with nothing on it, no house, just an old barn and Tom and Wailin bought my restored old colonial house on one and a quarter acres. For $8000 in 1973 this was a pure gift. Then a year later the land boom happened in the Coromandel and in six months the land had doubled its value. Then the Waikawau property sold very cheaply indeed and the $1000 raised from that was eaten up in five minutes by building this place. But how could I possibly move after 13 years of a slavish obsessional expenditure of energy crystallised into one acre of Brickellbrac?"

David Black remembers that Barry wanted more than anything to have a steam engine on his first railway. But the 10½-inch gauge line he had built was severely limited in its scope. This first railway became mainly a learning exercise, a plaything to put the milk bottles out and, as Barry was mostly using coal, not oil, to fire the kilns, the trucks were not as useful as they formerly had been in transporting drums of oil to the kilns. However, the train was invaluable for transporting truckloads of unglazed and glazed pots

TIM CHAMBERLAIN

to and from the salt glaze kiln on Sid Savill's property next door.

"I applied for an Arts Council grant in order to help with building the potteries here and I thought that if I had students here to teach pottery to they would look on my application more favourably. This is one of the reasons that I have had a number of students over the years learning here under my tuition, using my facilities, but I did not really want to teach pottery."

Helen Mason helped Barry dress for his appearance before the Arts Council committee considering his application and remembers that he wore a sports coat, tie and shoes. "I don't know where Barry got the shoes from." The whole Mason family were involved in assisting him to dress appropriately.

Barry is against formal dress in any form and shoes and ties particularly are anathema to him. On this occasion the eloquence of Dr Erskine and the unusually formal appearance of Barry in trousers and sports coat swayed the committee in his favour and they granted the funds he required to assist in the building of the potteries. He adds "I managed to get a second Arts Council grant later on to get better equipment and facilities."

The construction got underway: "The first thing I did was to have a flat area bulldozed out where the pottery stands. My next door neighbour Sid had a bulldozer. I used to do small engineering jobs for him and he would do jobs for me. I had a small engineering workshop, a welder and a lathe for building my own small trains that ran there. My former railway extended over his farm to a clay pit and a salt glaze, coal-fired kiln site which I had built. For the price of the diesel, Sid bulldozed the potteries site into two levels: the main level where the potteries are and a narrower upper level dug from a manuka scrub covered hillside. One day the council grader was diverted up here for the price of a few bottles of beer and just finished off the surface nicely."

The hillside was mostly grassy when Barry began to build. There were a few mature manuka trees but the site itself was relatively bare compared with today, where you can see young rimu and kauri saplings shooting up five metres or more into the sky.

"Then my apprentice Richard Brown started building an oil-fired kiln for us. The huge Star and Garter Hotel was being demolished in Coromandel township and that is how I got all the bricks for the kiln, from the chimneys of the big old hotel. I was sitting on the chimneys demolishing them and the same day those bricks were being used to build the kiln here. The bricks

Barry Brickell and Len Castle preparing to launch dinghy to board the Presto.

happened to be made out of a whitish burning clay and they did actually withstand the temperature of a stoneware glaze firing. We were lucky there — if they had been red bricks we couldn't have used them all through the kiln, just on the outside."

Barry bought the old steam launch the *Presto* in 1971. She had been the doctor's boat on the Waitemata Harbour and was later converted into a tug. She had been sitting without an engine, still rigged as a tug at an Auckland chandlers. He lashed her to the *St Lawrence* and the two boats slowly motored to Coromandel. Barry planned to install a steam engine to run the *Presto* as she had been when new. In the meantime, repainted and repaired with a diesel motor installed, the launch was used to haul building materials for the new Driving Creek Potteries. Barry transported loads of pots to sell in Auckland on the *Presto* and once took a load of several tons of clay to Whangarei to sell.

"My parents decided to demolish their house in Devonport and a demolition team and I worked together to take apart their house. I got truckloads of boards and wood, doors and windows, from the old family homestead, transported the wood over on the *Presto* and it was used in building the kitchen, and in sheds around the place. The gabled part of the kitchen was built first as a shed. I engaged a builder to do that. Then I built the wood-fired kiln next. It had never been done in New Zealand before, a wood-fired stoneware kiln. I have saved a part of this kiln for posterity."

The remains of this kiln sit close beside the railway line at the potteries. Moss and ferns grow inside it and slightly flawed terracotta pots and figurines sit outside. A sapling grows through the roof and the bricks sag gently as the clay slop that joins them slowly crumbles away in the moist air. This is another of Barry's 'gardens' that he allows to grow around him. He would hang string from taps to grow slime and algae, cultivate small travelling gardens of moss and ferns on his railway trucks; around his teacup and teapot outside the studio grows a yellow moss perfectly shaped to hold these two utensils which sit beside a tap across the railway line from his potter's wheel. He tells me that his ooze fountains were inspired by the richly coloured algal slime oozes which can sometimes be seen growing down Auckland's sandstone cliffs.

Jeff Scholes remembers: "Barry was a fabulous gardener. He bought a pile of native trees to plant on the property and I was impressed that he went to so much trouble. There was no vege gardening; Barry had large scale, long term concepts. I don't remember mowing any lawns — there wasn't much room for grass to grow. A goat looked after the orchard and systematically cleared it of blackberry. Everything was surfaced either with bricks or else it was railway.

"I built a room in the roof trying to make a bit of space for myself and put in the dormer windows — it is pretty amazing that Barry didn't mind me doing that. A lot of people see those dormer windows and imagine that the old villas had dormers but they hardly ever did. The pottery took up a large area of the house. The kitchen was warm but basic. The way Barry lived and what he did to the house had nothing to do with an original nineteenth century villa."

For the following year after he had sold the house to Wailin and Tom Elliott, Barry lived out of his old room in a corner of the house. When the new potteries could finally operate as a going concern he then had a hut built on the upper level as his own living quarters. The Elliotts gradually made the house suitable for a family to live in because Barry had not 'restored' the building in the accepted sense of the word but rather created a unique home combined with workshop for himself and the other potters who came to stay with him. Many walls had been removed over the years and some of these the Elliotts have replaced to give less open plan living. The bathroom, for example, was totally open plan because that suited Barry while he lived there.

The route of the railway may still be discerned in their garden but Barry lifted out almost all the rails and dismantled the viaduct that circled around the Norfolk pine. The first Driving Creek Railway was gradually removed and the years of experience used to build the new mountain railway on a much grander scale. For the first half of the 1970s Barry was too busy to do anything but survive the immense pressures to build the new potteries from scratch, make a living and pay for the construction work.

In 1973 the railway carriage was bought from the Mines Department at Rotowaro. He put in a successful tender of $125 each for two of them, Barry and David Black each buying one. They were superannuated coal miners' railway carriages built with longitudinal curved slatted seats rather like park benches, set opposite each other down each side. This was the style of old third class passenger carriages.

Barry remembers: "I spent three days at Rotowaro with the gas torch climbing around on black smutty grass cutting the bogies and wheels out from underneath the carriages." He had them railed to A & G Price Engineering in Thames and sold the bogies and wheels for scrap. "They were too big to use and I needed money, so I sold everything I could. Things I didn't need."

Then the carriages were taken to Coromandel separately on articulated flat-top truck units. To get Barry's carriage onto the site, they drove it up the driveway, jacked it up onto a crib-base and drove the truck out from underneath.

"Barry was very angry," David recalls, "because the guy who was driving the bulldozer kept lifting the carriage on parts that wouldn't take the strain and broke the brake wheel off."

David and Christine Black had bought 20 acres from Sid Savill on the hill above the potteries and wanted to put a house up there. It was a long way from the road and there was no electric power supply, no water or sewerage. Barry helped David get his house transported in pieces by barge from Auckland and to get the house to the top of the hill they winched it with a bulldozer onto the site and set it onto piles. The next challenge was to get the Black's railway carriage up there, and to get enough traction they dug the bulldozer into a metre deep hole and skidded the load up on its undercarriage. There it remains on the hilltop above Coromandel along with the house.

Later Barry had a bulldozer pull his carriage to its present site, jacked it up with large hydraulic jacks and set the foundations under it. It was subsequently transformed into a four bed bunkroom complete with electric power, sink

The Ngaru *was used to ferry pots to Auckland from 1987.*

and two desks by Philip Brown, a young man who was one of the 'hippies'. Barry describes him as "very diligent, frail and lost-looking". Philip lived at the potteries for some years and instead of becoming a potter, discovered the beauty of wood and became a very competent carpenter and woodworker. He became the mainstay builder at the potteries.

Barry had plans to fit a new steam engine and boiler to the *Presto* along with a ketch-rig to sail her. Sadly, these plans were not fulfilled. He took the *Presto* out of the water and stored her under cover for some time before deciding that he would have to sell her. He needed the money too desperately for building his railway and potteries and knew he could not do justice to the boat while he was so strapped for cash. The *Presto* was sold to Ralph Sewell in 1974 and Barry did not have a boat to use until he borrowed the *Ngaru* in 1987. By 1996 he was still using this launch, having recently completely refurbished her.

Barry later analysed his philosophy about the earliest days at the new Driving Creek Railway. He writes: "In 1973 I instigated a rural communal pottery workshop for simple approaches to craft pottery. No eligibility requirements were imposed. Sincerity and a commitment to the craft were requested as a condition to live and work at Driving Creek Potteries. Little selectivity based on experience was practised so this meant that there was a heavy reliance on trust and moral considerations. The building and running of the potteries was shared and food and pottery raw material costs were shared.

"The Arts Council contributed $3000 in late 1972. Apart from this funding, all capital expenses including buildings, plant, equipment and facilities were paid for by me. The old Catholic presbytery was given to us for demolition so we used the timber to build the two-storey pottery workshop, which became Coromandel's first pole and beam construction.

"I provided cheap accommodation for the potters who were in fact guests. No rent or board was charged; instead assistance to construct, establish and run the potteries was required. Donations of assets or materials towards the cause were welcome. Up to six potters were able to work at the potteries at once, if need be, each with their own work spaces.

"Firstly an oil-fired, drip-feed kiln was built and used for the first few years. Around 1974 a Dutch Oven wood-fired kiln of a larger size, single chamber downdraught, was built and used for glost firing. This kiln was the first wood-fired stoneware kiln in New Zealand and was built entirely from second-hand bricks. Both these kilns fired to stoneware temperatures. Then in 1975 a new and similar kiln with a 'bottle stack' was built by the guest potters and the old one retired from high temperature work.

"A 6 horsepower boiler was loaned to us for driving the pug mill and running a clay blunger on wood fuel. This was replaced in mid-1979 by a 15 horsepower Dispatch Foundry boiler of my own. Our workshop proved fairly productive and retailers would often drive over from various parts of the North Island to collect the pottery. During this period I felt unable to make much advancing work for exhibitions or commissions and I turned out a great deal of 'bread and butter' domestic ware, always under some pressure financially.

"The administration problems in effect left me with little time for 'creative' work. At times personality problems became very worrying. Overall the pottery turned out was of good quality with a basic emphasis on good form which was largely my interest. However, problems with the local clays and sometimes inadequate dry wood fuel gave us many headaches. It was found that the local clays suffered so much from siliceous content, causing dunting or brittleness, that a heavy reliance on clays from other parts of New Zealand was necessary.

"Although my aim was to be as self-reliant on local materials and fuels as possible, the costs of the requisite machinery for achieving this was beyond my means. Nevertheless I kept on acquiring all the second-hand machinery which I felt could benefit the potteries in the years to come and now I have a useful collection.

"A mechanical workshop was built, which has proved useful for repairing and maintaining the equipment which was installed at the potteries. This includes a light railway, 15-inch gauge, to facilitate the handling of wood fuel and clay materials."

Barry often had problems with members of the public visiting his potteries unannounced and he decided something about it. One of the stories of unexpected visitors is this: a station wagon full of nuns called in one day and found Barry potting naked, as he liked to do. They couldn't cope with the appearance of this nude man and ran back to their station wagon and disappeared. This sort of incident was just too inconvenient and annoying so Barry thought of an old railway enthusiast friend who could help and phoned him up. Merv Smith recalls:

"Barry rang me up once and said 'People seem to think that they can walk into my pottery and be shown around and have a ride on the train. Would you please tell people that this is not the case.'" So Merv did just that on his Auckland radio breakfast show.

"Then Barry sent me a DCR cup as a thank you gift and stamped into it is '6am 1070 KC narrow gauge steam coffee-rave bucket complements of Driving Creek Railway' and 'Please drive carefully' is pressed into the base. Barry sent it over to me saying 'This is a very good one'. Indeed it is a very good DCR railway mug. Light, delicate, a beautiful golden-orange in colour, a real treasure.

By 1975 Barry had a lot of young potters living and working at Driving Creek. They appeared to be taking over the place and Barry left for a holiday, telling them he didn't know when, but that he would be back.

He travelled to Dunedin where he stopped for five weeks and talked at length with Ralph Hotere, a good friend in need who advised Barry to pursue his own personal artistic growth. While he was there Barry built a very efficient kiln which burnt coal, wood and bark. In this he produced some pots, making use of locally available clay and minerals, which he found very exciting. He presented these to Ralph. Barry also told the Otago Polytech staff about the presence of these special local raw materials, but they were not very interested.

When Barry returned to the potteries several months later he found that the group he had left behind had substantially altered the kitchen, improving it greatly. They had built cupboards, made and installed the hand-adzed kauri table and pews and removed a wall, making the kitchen altogether roomier and more useful. It has remained largely unaltered since then.

Several couples formed among the young people at this time at Driving Creek Potteries and Barry was very uncertain about this. Since he lived a solo self-focused lifestyle he did not relate positively to the possibilities inherent in young people living and working together. He was apprehensive about these relationships forming and this fear is still with him today. His misgivings are groundless and many of the relationships which formed over the years between the young potters, artists and locals at the potteries have been lasting, productive and happy, an added benefit to the creativity fostered alongside the skills learned with Barry. He now admits he learned as much from them as they may have learned from him.

Until 1976, Barry was proud to state that he had never travelled outside New Zealand to study or pot. This was because he wanted to truthfully and faithfully capture the spirit of New Zealand in his work without outside influences intruding. Finally he did agree to travel and found it a very interesting and rewarding experience.

Hamish Keith relates the story behind Barry's travelling to the Edmonton Commonwealth Games in 1976. "I was then chairman of the Arts Council and we were asked to supply some financial support in sending Emily Schuster, a Maori weaver, to the Commonwealth Crafts Convention at Edmonton. I was sort of outraged that they were going to exploit a Maori artist again and portray them as NZ art. I persuaded the Council to send a pakeha artist as well and it was decided at very short notice. We decided, without asking him, to send Barry Brickell. So I phoned Barry — and this is an example of his simultaneously cunning and naive approach to the world.

"I said, Barry, we'd like you to go the Games."

"Oh I'm not very good at games," Barry replied.

"No, you dummy, the crafts convention in Edmonton."

"I haven't got anything to wear."

"Well we'll give you some money for clothes."

"Oh — can I see my sister who lives over there?"

"Yes, Barry, we will give you some money for that and to cover your other expenses."

So we approved some funds for Barry and Air New Zealand agreed to carry them both first class. When it came time to leave, Barry turned up at my place for me to take him to the airport with a flax kit, old corduroy trews, a T-shirt and sandals. So I asked him:

"Barry, what did you do with the money for the clothes?"

"Oh — something came up with the railway," he said.

"So Barry went off and had a whale of a time at Edmonton and charmed everybody there."

This was his first trip overseas and he was away for three months. He toured the USA on a slim budget and stayed with his friends Max and Barbara Gimblett in New York. He says he found it rather hot in North America and bought clothes when he needed them. ("You can't wear shorts there," he recalls, "it's all tight jeans and strict pop conventions.")

From this beginning full of hard construction work, things progressed at the potteries and Barry established a reputation as a craftsman teacher. He is quoted in *Art in Schools*, an Education Department publication, saying "I do not presume to teach or change people who come here. It is entirely up to them to make the best of it for all; themselves, me, and anyone else. I cannot educate: I am far too busy with my own work. People educate themselves when they are fulfilled and happy in their work. There is no such thing as teaching: only learning."

In 1977 there were seven potters — six men and one woman — working alongside Barry. Driving Creek Potteries were styled 'a rural handcraft workshop'. The lives of the potters there involved using all the machinery as adjuncts to the handcraft of potting. Everyone had a share in supplying food, shelter, gardening, building, clay making, plumbing, cooking, firing the kilns and preparing the pine wood fuel for the firings. As is usual with human nature the potters would often have to be pressured into the less attractive tasks.

There were three wood-fired kilns and one oil-fired which was to be dismantled soon. Because all kilns are built with clay slop and little cement they are easily dismantled and the old bricks, if still suitable, may be cleaned and recycled into a new kiln.

"I don't know how many hundreds of kilns I have built and how many hundreds I have pulled down," Barry says gleefully. His enjoyment of channelling fire to his and others' uses know no bounds. Many people over the years have asked Barry to build or alter kilns for them. Yvonne Rust and

The first viaduct on the new Driving Creek Railway line was completed in 1978 and provided easy access to terracotta clay and pine wood fuel from the property.

Barry would fight over kiln building, shouting at each other nose to nose and cracking bricks with the force of their argument carried through the hammer.

Along with all this ceaseless activity and the enormous effort required to completely build Driving Creek Potteries on an entirely undeveloped site, the railway was not forgotten.

Barry continues: "In 1978 a 150-foot long viaduct was completed which gave us access to more terracotta clay and wood fuel from the property. From the start, terracotta (planters, terrace ware etcetera) has been a substantial proportion of our output. As well some thousands of red bricks have been hand moulded for use in kiln building.

"In all, the experience gained in building up the potteries from scratch and sharing ideas and problems with the other potters has been rewarding. One thing it all brought home to me was that my efforts at administration were not very successful and my own directional work in clay had suffered."

CHAPTER FIVE

A NEW LINE
1979-1996

"We speak too often with confusion about art and craft. If I were to suggest that every person born has his or her unique nature and way of doing a particular thing, I could be accused of promoting individualism, yet this is a fundamental condition for art. Why do many people have such a strong desire to conform, to trap themselves in a particular style or outlook which limits their freedom? If art is to craft as how is to thing then every time we do something innocently in our own quiet way we could be committing a work of art."

– Barry Brickell

For Barry, 1979 was a momentous year, a black year according to some, when he did not want to know anyone. It was a year in which he reassessed his philosophy regarding the way in which he had managed or mismanaged the environment around him and then made the appropriate changes so that at the present day the potteries are unrecognisable to those who lived with him during the 1970s and up until 1980.

He wrote down for himself his ideas as they were evolving. These changes were partly a consequence of his international travel for three months in the USA and Canada after the Edmonton Commonwealth Games and his thoughts about the world and his place in it. Here are some of his musings, which are more those of a man who knows his failings and strengths and needs than those of an arrogant, difficult artist.

"During the past few years I had been having all the normal apprehensions which result from mixed loyalties. Towards my own personal craft development and towards the other people living on my property to whom I felt obliged in various ways.

(Right) An example of Barry Brickell's trackwork, in the yards at DCR. He considers his best railway construction to be the highest, most recent section, where the degree of difficulty and his decades of experience produced his most satisfying result.

PHOTOGRAPH: TIM CHAMBERLAIN

"Since my return from Canada and the USA last year, I have seen a greater benefit in the potential of shared cultural pursuits on an international basis, than in simply encouraging a lifestyle supposedly based on a handcraft. The excitement of being able to put the crafts to a valid and vital use in our rather brash culture has started to mean more to me than merely an 'alternative' to the conventional lifestyles of New Zealand.

"In order to carry out these ideals I must get my house in order first. This must involve a complete reshuffle of people, amenities, equipment and attitudes, especially towards work. I plan to have only those people at the potteries who can prove to me that it is the best workshop for them to come to for a specific project. In selecting more carefully the most committed potters in terms of pottery craft or other relevant activities, I should be relieved of much administrative work. In order to retain the usefulness and value of Driving Creek Potteries, both to those who work there and to the community, I must try to encourage its use rather more for those who have specific projects or have a deep sense of commitment to their craft rather than just enjoying the lifestyle it provides.

"This enhanced criticality has more chance of reaching out in other ways into the community and it could also be a much needed starting point for cultural exchange. Since my return from America after last year's three month trip I realise now that a true cultural exchange can only take place during the sharing of work. Thus I see the need to offer workshop space and facilities of a higher standard than I have managed to provide so far. At the same time I do not see my part as having to cater for an international standard of techniques or attitudes towards the craft. We have in New Zealand a potential for innovation and vitality every bit as great as that in other countries. The 'grass growing greener' overseas is a total, utter and complete myth.

"Now, with ultra-fast communication and lessening cultural inequities, the nature and ability and dignity of every individual is of increasing importance. I see this as an essential complement to industrialisation, not as antagonistic to it. To get my house in order, I need to tackle the various 'jack-ups' and half-completed projects at Driving Creek Potteries. This involves improving the facilities with which we must work, weatherproofing, organising the raw materials and fuel supplies, storage and preparation areas so that all are more efficient. The elements of uncertainty in these areas in the past have slowed much progress and dulled enthusiasm.

Bush railways were traditionally used to extract timber from New Zealand's remote hill country. Barry has reversed the convention by using his railway to replant the property in native trees. Shown here with Megan Wilson, Peter Hills, and members of the Forest and Bird Protection Society, 1988.

"I do not intend to provide anything other than the necessary basics with which to work properly and in some ways a note of austerity must remain. The Arts Council has decided, without my application, to assist these causes, which although relieving me of a difficult financial burden, places an obligation in the sense of ultimate benefit to the community. So now I see the continuation of a shared workshop principle, while refining it in various ways in order to make definite advances in the craft rather than being content with 'subsistence'. While this will not relieve me of administrative duties entirely, it should certainly render them more bearable, even attractive and interesting.

"My own studio has a right to resume its former vitality, even greater than when working alone. I hope to virtually eliminate the various inhibitions, communication breakdowns and authoritarianism into which I have been forced by the situation at Driving Creek Potteries in the past. While the design of the studios will allow complete working and living privacy the shared jobs and chores will remain an important part of the life of a craftsperson at Driving Creek. There will be space for up to two guest potters in the new arrangement. My raw material preparation machinery will remain available for the use of other potters. Being very comprehensive and having cost much time, energy and money, the machinery should serve as many as possible who need it.

"The context is important, however. I am basically committed to my studio work and have no desire to enter into any kind of commercial activity with my machinery. It will be set up to serve as and when needed by the potters. The old plant has worked well in this way but the new plant will be much more comprehensive. It will include heavy crushing and grinding gear as well as a brick making machine, pug mill, ball mills and blunger.

"There is a need to break down the confusion that seems to have always existed between 'artist' and machine. Machines need have no more power over humanity than does any hand tool and this is the sense in which I see it: machinery has its place as well as its poetry. We no longer must live in an age of subservience other than to our fellow human beings. The whole beauty of the cultural world lies in the elimination of power systems which inevitably suppress, oppress and repress the human spirit. Our machinery, skills and outlook must remain subservient to human needs, remain a strictly cultural activity and not aggressively compete with industry (by advertisement, persuasion etc). Only in this way will our workshops avoid the stifling cloak of institutionalism, the like of which has tended to pervade the Christian Church.

"If this has seemed like some sort of deviation from the description of a pottery workshop project, I see a great need to lay down the conditions to

Young potters from Vanuatu working at Driving Creek, 1983. Barry had earlier tutored their group in Vanuatu and they built a kiln under his direction.

ensure its future vitality. The conditions are really attitudes; we may say that it is not the *thing* but *how*."

Barry wrote this in 1979, responding to his own internal changes and growth in his ideas about the why and wherefore of his activities on his land. He then began changing the emphasis of the activities at DCR and gradually the situation evolved into a paired guest potter situation with others visiting and working but living outside the potteries.

In 1978 Barry began a brief series of his own summer gatherings. He entitled them 'Potters Doos', and focused them around the old cowshed and barn where everyone ate and 60 or 70 people, potters and their friends and families would come to stay at Driving Creek for a week of free camping and socialising in January. It was a great idea but didn't work as a teaching arena because the demands of children on the parents prevented continuous learning, but it was terrific as a social week in the middle of summer for old friends to meet and fire the kiln together and talk over old times. Sadly, too many gatecrashers and hangers-on who were not interested in pottery began to invade the 'Doo' and Barry decided to stop hosting them. The last 'Doo' was held in 1981. "The teacher personality, the guru, is gone," Barry said later.

In 1980 he was given the commission to make a mural to celebrate the centenary of the Waitaki NZ Refrigeration Company. The mural was to be hung in their head office in Christchurch. The Queen Elizabeth Arts Council had been consulted on the best artist to choose for this commission and Barry was the fortunate sculptor selected.

Once his design and plan had been accepted Barry asked David Black, by now an accomplished photographer and medical practitioner, to accompany him to the large freezing works at Imlay in Wanganui. There they spent a whole day together taking hundreds of photographs, attempting to record the essence of each working man's job on the chains and in other parts of the freezing works. Some of the photographs were encapsulated into the relief terracotta tiles Barry made and included in the mural.

He also asked Barry Lett to assist him with the mural. "Another aspect of my association with Barry was that he asked my advice over the Waitaki freezing works mural," Barry Lett recalls. "As well as having the clay relief work, he was going to paint areas on canvas and cloth and I had been work-ing on cotton duck, so I exchanged a few ideas with him over that and a little while later he came around and gave me a fruit bowl as a thank you gift. If

Barry needs information on something he will go to someone and not only get the information, but often get them to do it for him!"

That year Barry met John Matthews and his life changed forever. John is a businessman based in New Plymouth. They met through Barry's large ambitious exhibition held at and commissioned by the Govett Brewster Art Gallery in September 1980 called *Baroque Politocaust*. The exhibition featured 40 sculptured terracotta clay forms exhibited with steam flowing through them in a setting of native plants. Barry laid out 12 steam holes which steamed up through gravel into the exhibition pots which were placed over them. John supplied a steam cleaner to provide the steam. Unfortunately it blew up and a big search went on in New Plymouth until a 1947 Anderson upright boiler was found, hired and tended lovingly by Barry.

Barry's sister Andrea, with her husband Robert Oliver, played live baroque music while the steam hissed through the exhibition. The Govett Brewster bought four of Barry's pieces: *Torsomorph*, *Taxodon*, *Symetromorph lugged*, and *Businomorph II*.

John Matthews remembers the exhibition: "It was a strange counterpoint — because here you have Barry with all this steam and his wonderful organic strange shapes outside with all of them hissing steam, a bit of smoke and a lot of action. Wonderfully organic stuff going on and inside his sister and brother-in-law playing really very pristine chamber music.

"Barry and I have a mutual empathy with New Zealand native plants. We have the biggest collection in New Zealand here at our New Plymouth home of New Zealand native plants. I have more than one and a half thousand different native species so we get a kick out of that and Barry gets a kick out of it so when we are up at DCR or when he's down here, in Taranaki, there's lots of common interest.

"In fact we invited Barry down, I remember now, and he stayed with us for a couple of days. During the evening we were talking as we were sitting on the sofa and we got to the point about commissioning a work and the dialogue we had was:

"Barry, would you like to do a commission? I asked and his reaction was

"Oh dear, oh dearie me...! Oh dearie me, I'm not too sure about this — proposition." And he got quite squirmy on the sofa then he said:

"It would depend on what sort of work you would want."

"So I said to him, 'Well, it would be anything that you wanted to do. Had a passion to do — had a real dream about doing.' So he became much more excited about that.

"'Oh my! Goodness gracious!' And so we reflected on what it might be — something about steam engines and locomotives... he was talking about doing at one stage, as a commission for an art gallery, the driving cab of a steam engine. It was all in terracotta and you could go in and turn valves and pull knobs and levers and have steam and all the necessary noises emerging from this living sculpture. But he didn't want to do this project for us, he ranged over other subjects and then he asked:

"Well — how big should this be?" and I said:

"'Well, any size, but if you need a size, let's say as big as the sofa that you are sitting on.' Barry got very excited about that too.

"Goodness gracious, this sounds a magnificent opportunity!"

"Then we got round to the sensitive part about how much it might cost and I suggested that perhaps it would cost so much and he thought that was OK, we agreed on that. Then, normally with a commission, we will get the drawings and then the maquette (model) and then the full size art work but in this case we didn't do that. Barry went away and we just left him to it. I had enough confidence to leave him to produce whatever he wanted which we have seldom done with any other artist.

"Then the commission went through a huge gestation period; from memory it was like two years of gestation. I remember Hamish Keith calling me once. He had been staying with Barry and Hamish said to me:

"My goodness, do you have any idea what he's building for you?" and I replied:

"'No, I haven't any idea, Hamish.' And he said:

"'It's a sofa with rivets all over it!' because he'd heard, from Barry, about the sofa! And I thought, Oh well, this will be exciting! This is a novel idea! and left it at that, and then, of course, we started getting communications from Barry about how it was evolving:

Dear John,   DCR 28/1/81

Just thinking about your sculptural terracotta conchomorph. I'm having ideas while working on the Waitaki Co mural. On this job I have been working from photos, especially the killing chain series, modelling in deep relief men at work at their allotted tasks. I have found that I am quite able to work in human 'semi-portraiture'.

This leads me to think a little of your project. I think it would be a fine idea if I could 'embellish' the surfaces with 'scenes' derived from your engineering works. Welding, cutting, doing up bolts, fitting, turning and spray painting are all splendid activities. Perhaps I ought to get some photos of activities around your works sometime.

My present work is flat tiles which fit together to form panels. The mind fair boggles at what could be done, in your case. Although my present work is depicatory rather than 'abstract' I feel this is of no consequence. The basic form is the main thing.   — *Barry*

Dear John,   DCR 3/8/81
Just a kindly, friendly, combined safety valve cum blowdown advice note that all six separate sections of the 'Locomorph' stove unit are now completed and the blacksmith is getting ready to accept them into his 'stress relieving' furnace in about a week's time.

Advice will be forthcoming by phone, of the results.

Following good results you will be cordially invited to attend the assembling campaign which will be conducted in great secrecy (from the media) and attended with much blowing. If all goes well it could be a great work.
Cheerfully (at this stage)   — *Barry*

"Then three days later Barry writes again: 'This chance taken to inform you that your 'Locomorphic Rivettocotta' will be subjected to the grand treatment (stress relieving furnace) next Thursday. Hopefully all will be well but kilns are great ruiners of mankind's best endeavours. Humbling. We will see if I too, in God's opinion, need stress relieving.'"

John continues: "So he told us it was coming together and it was looking great and it was formed and then air-dried and then fired and then prepared ready and then finally it was ready for us to go and look at it and we made an expedition to go up to Driving Creek Railway and found this marvellous steam engine. It is a wonderful work, a splendid work.

"There's a touch of reality in it because it looks quite real to some people. My father in his older age on some occasions thought it *was* real. And there's lovely humour in it, because round the back side of it, Barry has created in the terracotta a little area of welding as if this was a steam engine that had a fault; it is as if someone had welded and repaired it. There is also a steam generator which goes in it which every now and again lets off a slight shooshing noise and a little puff of steam comes out the top."

An additional joke in that little terracotta 'weld' is that it is the sort of fault in a boiler which would cause it to be condemned by a Marine Department inspector, because it is a welded crack running out from a rivet hole in what should be a flawless plate.

This was the first of several works John Matthews has commissioned from Barry Brickell and it effectively launched a new era of his creativity.

Helen Mason, potter and founding editor (1958-67) of NZ Potter, *lives in her house truck at Driving Creek Potteries, where she has her own workshop.*

Jeff Scholes comments: "In the 1960s we had a passion and excitement to pot even though we knew it had all been done before. There was a sense of creativity and discovery that was part of the creative process. Barry is important because of his pioneering — it is something that is in everybody, a sense of excitement and romance. Potters should represent that kind of romance. It is epitomised in someone like Barry, especially with the railway as well. As potters we had a thirsty public, hungry for interesting objects. Crown Lynn had a monopoly in a protected industry at the time. There had been many commercial potteries but they disappeared in Crown Lynn's wake."

Barry has continually maintained the pioneering romance and drama. During the 1980s he was busy with commissions for terracotta sculptures, domestic ware and the extension of the railway. It took two years for the double-decker viaduct to be built and it was finished in 1991 with great celebration. It was the last bridge necessary to finish the railway and since it has been completed 'Hoki Mai', a main station and barbecue area and an arboretum featuring native shrubs have been constructed. In the latter part of 1994 and early 1995 the last switchback on the line was completed at 'Cascade' and now the railway line has raced up the hillside along the 20-year-old

Dr Deirdre Airey was one of the first to befriend Barry at Coromandel. She now makes modelled terracotta relief tiles.

surveyed route and reached the ridge top 'Terminus' in the year of Barry's 60th birthday. He was pleased to finish laying the main line after 33 years of almost continuous railway construction.

Barry taught at the Northland Craft Trust Summer Doo in January 1987. Yvonne Rust had asked Barry if she could use his title of 'Doo' for her summer schools after his had finished.

Helen Mason called in to see her old friend; she found herself stranded between homes because she had sold her place in Tokomaru Bay and her house truck was not yet finished. Barry was alone and Helen asked if she could come to stay indefinitely until her house truck was ready. She remembers: "He didn't say yes and he didn't say no so I stayed. I then decided that the least I could do was make sure Barry had one decent meal a day."

Helen has continued to do this, cooking most nights, and in early 1996 she celebrated her 81st birthday. She now lives permanently at the potteries in her house truck, potting: making fountains and some domestic ware, tending her herb garden and looking after herself. She has also been instrumental in setting up the Tauira Toru Craft Trust which operates on land which it owns adjacent to Driving Creek Railway and Potteries.

In 1987 an old friend, Murray Norman, inventor of the Newmarket Car Fair two decades earlier, offered to buy kiln loads of Barry's domestic ware, taking the pots and sculptures to resell in Auckland. He gave Barry cash for the pots he bought and organised an area in his brother's carpet factory in Carbine Road, Mount Wellington, as a retail space. He would then retail the pots for twenty percent above what he had paid Barry.

Murray says "I felt that Barry's work was so valuable to people. I felt that not only I had to have it but pottery lovers had to have Barry's pots too. I

(Opposite) Barry Brickell in action at the 1987 Northland Craft Trust Summer Doo, with Yvonne Rust.

didn't mind if the pots did sell, but I didn't mind if they didn't; it was a hobby for me. People got lots of pleasure out of the pots. I love Barry's work."

Murray organised The Pot Place weekend sales three times each year. "Carbine Road was way off the beaten track but 'Brickell lovers' would find it. All it took was one or two ads in the *Herald*. Often there were a dozen people waiting for the doors to open when they would charge in to see what they could buy from the latest firing and red SOLD stickers would quickly be everywhere. I love Barry's domestic ware; he's famous for his coffee mugs, and he will be remembered for them in a hundred years' time."

These 'Pot Place' sales of Brickell domestic ware may well have been the last firings of domestic ware that Barry will ever make for sale. He has always been reluctant to see himself as a maker of coffee mugs and a comment was made that "seeing Barry work on domestic ware is like seeing an elite engineer working on a Belmont." In the blurbs advertising The Pot Place Barry complained about making coffee mugs and admitted having nightmares about making them. On the *Kaleidoscope* programme Peter Coates produced, Barry also had a moan about making domestic ware but then he says "I love complaining about having to make domestic ware, but secretly I thoroughly enjoy it when I can make it for friends and not for sale."

Because of the railway's success, it is unlikely that any more coffee mugs or any of those other favourite Brickell domestic items, like fatso jugs, thinsos or the classic quango pots (named after government committees, these sinuous pots looked as if they held water but in fact had a big hole in the bottom) will be produced for bread and butter reasons alone. The conditions will have to be right and now, at last, Barry is able to become a hobby potter once again.

Murray Norman also believes that Barry's *Stations of the Cross* relief tile series is his best work and laments that it ended up above the cafeteria servery at Nga Tapuwae College in Mangere for a while until he and Barry visited and requested that the series be moved into the library. Terracotta is a very absorbent material and smoke and cooking fumes must have affected the tiles. Barry discovered the concept of the 14 stations of the cross through his friend Deirdre Airey, developed his own understanding of the story and equated it with 14 of the stations on the North Island main trunk line.

Barry Brickell appeared in the New Year Honours List for 1987, awarded the Order of the British Empire for services to Pottery. John Matthews recalls *(Opposite)* The Snake *as Bullet Train.*

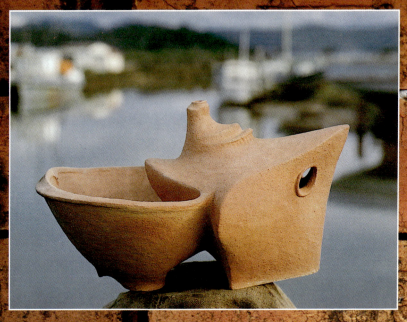

(Top) *Boat sculpture in terracotta.* (Above) *A love for old machinery.*

PHOTOGRAPHS: STEVE RUMSEY

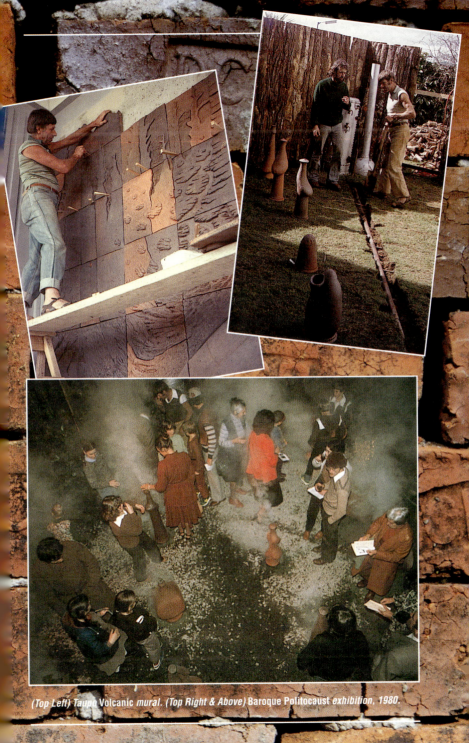

(Top Left) Taupo Volcanic *mural. (Top Right & Above)* Baroque Politocaust *exhibition, 1980.*

Examples of Barry Brickell's early domestic ware.

From **The Stations of the Cross** *series, 1985.*

(Top) The railway builder. (Above) Detail from spiral cutting. (Right) **The Snake** *on double-deck viaduct.*

the investiture ceremony the following May:

"Well that was a *great* adventure. At the time of the investiture, Barry chose me to be one of the guests. We found out what the dress protocols were, that he had to wear black dinner dress and black shoes. We made arrangements to hire a dinner suit. Then when he arrived in Wellington we sort of put Barry into the suit. That went pretty well, it was a bit tight but we got him into it, and then came the point about the shoes. He has got about size 12 or 13 feet, very organic feet, we had already let Barry know that he had to bring a pair of shoes. He turned up with this paper bag and out came these pair of suede fawn shoes, size 12 or 13 and we looked at these with astonishment and said:

"Barry you can't wear fawn suede shoes to an investiture with a dinner suit and jacket and so on, it's just not appropriate." He got very, very anguished about this, and we all did, indeed, because we didn't have much time so we did a frantic phone around the shoe shops of Wellington to see if anybody had a pair of size 12 or 13 black shoes and no one had. So we were stuck with these fawn things and to solve the problem we rushed into the city, got some shoe dye, dyed his suede shoes to a black suede and went off to the investiture with the shoes still somewhat damp. It was a great adventure, Barry loved every second of it and so did I. A great adventure, a lot of fun."

Wellington dealer Peter McLeavey wanted to have an exhibition of Barry's work in 1992 and they decided upon the theme *Resurrection of The Goddess*. In response to this Barry 'preened his bachelor tufts' and created a series of the most sensuo-erotic terracotta coiled sculptures he had yet produced. Most of the sculptures are more than four feet high. They collectively and singly awe the viewer with their power and energy. Barry fired them in his huge up-downdraught kiln which he designed to give even firing temperatures throughout, as well as beautiful wood ash 'flashing' effects on the sculptures inside.

By 1996 there were seven kilns at Driving Creek Potteries: the remains of the first kiln, a gas-fired kiln, an oil-fired kiln and three wood-fired kilns. Helen Mason has her own small gas-fired kiln. From the Dispatch 15 hp boiler there are no less than five steam-powered engines connected by steam pipes. These engines were collected by Barry from all over New Zealand, some from factories, some from old ships, one from the dredge *Eileen Ward* and others from gasworks or sawmills.

Sadly, on 18 January 1995, Barry's own studio burned to the ground with

(Left) Chipman's Junction, Driving Creek: the timeless allure of a New Zealand bush railway.

PHOTOGRAPHS PG 103, 104: TIM CHAMBERLAIN

the greater part of his personal diary and photograph collection. He describes it as a 'vicious intense fire' which happened while the potters and their friends were having dinner. He concentrated on his railway for the rest of the year, vowing to return to his potting in 1996.

The fire was a tragedy but at least the other buildings and the bush clad hills were spared, as there had been a heavy downpour the day before.

Apart from Helen Mason and Barry, two professional potters live and work in separate studios on the premises. Friends and visitors come and go continuously. It is Barry's energy and vision which draws them to Coromandel.

Barry has plans for a new studio and for rebuilding the main house, externally sheaved in terracotta moulded blocks and bricks. The upper storey will contain a gallery of his private art collection. He spends several hours each day in the early morning or late evening on track work, alone, and progresses quickly. He lays ballast under the sleepers, straightening and laying the rails and tying them to the sleepers. The roar of the cascade in the creek accompanies him while the bellbirds, tuis and fantails sing and fly about the bush through which the narrow ribbon of the track runs. The Grand Scheme is nearing completion and since the rails reached the level area of the summit on 21 June 1995, the railway's passengers have been able to enjoy the view in just the way Barry has envisaged for the past 25 years.

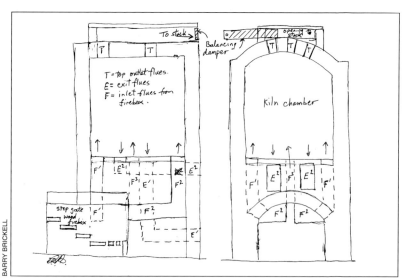

Big multi-flue kiln for firing large terracotta pieces. A balanced updraught-downdraught design, 1988.

CHAPTER SIX

'RADIOACTIVE'

"Radioactive areas are very scary places and need to be treated with huge respect."
— Barry Brickell

Whenever I engage in a discussion about Barry, his life and history, invariably and often unexpectedly the topic of his sexuality will occur. My interviewees will earnestly or scoffingly, loudly or softly tell me exactly what *they* think about Barry and the way he has chosen to live his life, sexually.

Even Barry's father Maurice, at the venerable age of 84, declared loudly that I should know that Barry has never touched a woman all his life. A fact that seems to stun Maurice Brickell while also fascinating him. It is as well Maurice was not influenced in a similar way or else Barry would never have been born.

A more typical conversation would go something like this. I will make a statement saying that essentially, so far as I could ascertain to that date, Barry has been celibate and essentially a virgin all his 60 years. The listener may then say something like "Well, that's not true. I heard that a young woman got into Barry's bed and seduced him in the 1960s/70s. Mind you, I wasn't there. You will have to ask someone else if that is true." Then they will suggest someone who they believe knows more about this incident. The person suggested will invariably know nothing about the supposed incident and I go back to my original statement.

I have kept an open mind about all this dialogue and listened patiently to all manner of views — many made and then contradicted.

Sometimes letters arrive with comments like this from Elwyn Richardson: "In a way, I think Barry's sexuality is a hell of a lot simpler than any have thought. I don't think he's ever had a lover. He's certainly not had sexual intercourse with anyone. I don't believe that he's been even remotely entertained by the idea of a homosexual union. He probably wouldn't even recognise

such a bring-on. I believe he's a genuine innocent. A sort of god-like person, like Shelley or Rupert Brooke or Keats. A romantic in that original sense. Eating off his environment. Barry shows so much innocence!"

Other friends of Barry will tell me that although they have lots of information about his personal life, they won't tell me what they know and I am not permitted to write about his personal relationships. Which leaves me with many mysteries. Why is there so much to be said about a man who has made a simple and allowable choice for himself which harms nobody?

Often Barry himself will suddenly comment upon his life history saying something like "I remember that my penis was not a penis for a long time, not until I was quite old — it was a 'downere'. At the same time I was trying to get an explanation of why it went up and down, stiff and not so stiff. I can't remember what the explanation was."

This sort of parental reticence was typical of the pre-World War Two generations and not unusual. It would have been unusual if Barry's parents had educated him about his body and sexual potential. Eventual sexual activity, after marriage only, was an accepted thing and a married couple kept their problems with intimacy to themselves.

Perhaps no one can say, least of all Barry, if a decision was ever made that he would never engage in sexual activity with either sex. He subscribes to the belief, one held by certain Chinese philosophers, and many in the Indian sub-continent, that sexual activity takes away from the energy, creativity and life force of the male individual.

Lois McIvor, an old student friend, says "Barry says he is living a celibate life and I never imagined he did otherwise. His obsession with creativity channels the energy into his work. Other people get in the way... Barry was always very shy and lacking in social graces towards women. He would never flirt or indulge them in chat. In fact he was sort of 'clumsy' in a way."

John Matthews has had many friendly bawdy debates with Barry about sex and art and he says that Barry is and always has been intensely interested in what happens, from a physical and intellectual standpoint, but that because of this conviction about the potential losses to his art and energy, he has never allowed himself to indulge in physical intimacy with another human being, even when the emotional and physical opportunity has been available.

(Opposite) The sculpture garden at Driving Creek: "I like rich animated forms, not bawdy, offensive or sexy contriva".

PHOTOGRAPH: TIM CHAMBERLAIN

John comments: "I think that Barry has always emphatically maintained a distance from having a sexual relationship with anybody and very vigorously repelled any advances. He's mentioned it to us on occasions that for him it would be a... transgression, an adventure of great folly. He has said 'Oh! it would be terrible, I could end up being totally distracted and totally put on the wrong tracks! I'd be going up the wrong line', because he likes to speak figuratively about sex. Barry has made comments that to have a sexual relationship could be quite a destructive diversion of all his energies when he wants to get on with the Grand Scheme of doing the Work."

This disinterest and celibacy has affected Barry's relationships with many people he has met, especially those women who came to be friends with him, sometimes living at Driving Creek. Some of them attempted to seduce Barry, loving him, caring for him, charmed by his innocence and smile, muscles and intellect and most of all by the incredibly sensual ceramics he makes.

To look at the breasts and buttocks that appear magically bursting through the skins of Barry's peopillics and businomorphs, vaginal openings and those fascinating little nipples and holes organically growing out of his terracotta, anyone would reasonably think that Barry Brickell could be the most sensual man alive. Some have gone further and applied this assumption to their relationship with Barry.

David Black, who saw the engineering side of him, comments that he sees Barry as interested in sex on a first principles basis, much as we would be interested in bridge building or gasworks construction. Barry hated being pursued as a 'challenge' by women and would run away very fast if pursued. At the same time, he was attracted to women. When David spent eight months living at Driving Creek he helped Barry build more line to his new kilns. Barry watched with interest David's relationships with his girlfriends.

There are stories of women being thrown out of Driving Creek for attempting to seduce Barry. I do not doubt that this is true. If rejected by a man a woman may feel angry, humiliated and suspect his manhood. In the past and to an extent in the present too, asexual people have been accused and suspected groundlessly of homosexuality. Naturally Barry does not relish these situations and at times he has escaped into hiding and been very unhappy and uncomfortable with these assumptions made about him.

Potters tend to keep very fit and muscular and Barry is no exception. He has also spent a good deal of his adult life virtually naked. He would wear

Brickell believes that sexual activity reduces the energy, creativity and life force of the male. His sculptural works reveal a fascination with the sensuality of human forms.

cut-off shorts that were completely lacking a crotch and held together by elastic or string. Denis Hanna remembers: "When Barry would bend over stacking the kiln all his genitals would hang out the back but he didn't mind. If you were visiting Barry you could see all his works." His near-nudity became a feature of the potteries for his many visitors, to which they adjusted so completely that now they are shocked to see him in standard issue shorts or jeans.

Denis continues: "No one had ever met anyone like Barry. There were so many sides to him and so many people rolled into one."

He used to have talks about sex with Joy Hanna, telling her: "If it came to the point I'd know how to do it but I'm not homosexual, I'm asexual, I'm just not interested." His garden objects are very sexual. He models the vulva and the breast. It's curious where all this comes from."

Barry has now acquired a form of physical modesty in keeping with his role as a tourist railway operator and nothing shockingly nude may be seen at DCR any more. Barry has told me he does his best work naked and he has shared this with other artists like Tony Fomison and a young man who, I am told, would set up his potter's wheel on the roof and throw pots, working naked in the Coromandel sunlight.

Women in Barry's age group were socialised to view single men as a potential meal ticket, husband and father material. Even now he is at pains to explain to me that he is 'not an eligible bachelor' and I see how different life is today from the 1950s when Barry grew up and white virgin weddings were the desired norm.

The Fairburn and Beck children were all friends in the same social group when Barry was a teenager and one evening he took out a group of couples, with himself as the single, unpartnered driver, to the movies, or 'the pictures' as it was then called. Janis Fairburn tells of how Barry annoyed them immensely by rounding up all the girls afterwards and insisting upon delivering them straight to their homes instead of remaining as they had intended in Takapuna to dally with their boyfriends and make their own way home. This story has survived 40 years and is still laughingly retold as one of the legends about Barry Brickell. Everyone realised then that Barry did not truly understand what boy-girl relationships were about, or, if he did, he certainly did not relate to those feelings at all. He did not appear to notice the others of his own age group having adult relationships. This was not important or significant to him. The whereabouts of feldspar pegmatite and good stoneware clay bodies or an old coal mine were what really caught Barry's imagination.

Denis Hanna remembers: "Barry was besieged by all these people coming to watch the firings, gawk at him and play music so he needed somewhere to escape to study and he used to come over and study in our back room off our lounge." Barry would bicycle over to study his botany and geology papers in a tiny room in the Hannas' home.

While Hamish Keith and Len Castle had girlfriend after girlfriend and shared naughty jokes with each other and Terry Barrow, Barry listened with amazement, boredom and disgust. He did not understand why this sort of behaviour was interesting or amusing.

At the time when others in his age group were marrying and having children he decided to move to Coromandel. There, having bought the old schoolhouse, Barry painfully came to the realisation that he had a responsibility the equal of 'a wife and children'. The first Driving Creek property took up a great deal of his energy and he never had any time to think of anything other than earning an income, building his first railway and restoring the old kauri house.

Since that time Barry has evolved from making domestic ware into making terracotta sculptures. He still makes domestic ware, but less and less often. These sculptures are built up laboriously by hand coiling them and the shapes and ideas come from the unconscious as they grow through Barry's hands. He can and does channel the way the shapes form and when commissions come in he makes the ordered pieces in styles altered from the usual products of his hands. Shirley Brickell commented to me: "Remember that tall fountain at Ravington Junction in the pool? It started out to be a totara tree and ended up covered in breasts!" She is amused rather than flummoxed by her elder son's fixation on the female human form.

Barry's sister Romilly is slightly embarrassed by her big brother's obsession with the sexual body parts of the human being. She sees this fascination as a reflection of the conflict within her brother of their parents' Victorian values and the true sexual feelings Barry has.

So I ask Barry and he says: "I have never had a sexual drive — not a bit. Bored by it from an early age." To me this is a genuine statement. He seems totally honest, actually and intuitively, as he coils part of another sculpture and prepares for another stint working up the line.

Once he wrote: "I am speaking as an outsider to the culture in which I live... I am unmarried, and never had any interest in being married. I have had no sexual or social desire and am a natural celibate. I am like a hermit in a sense and my energy goes into the things I do with my hands."

Barry admits that yes, one or two women did indeed get into bed with him and attempted to seduce him on widely separated occasions but: "I just wanted a quiet night's sleep and I was dumped into a situation where I didn't choose to be dumped and I had to get out of it. Indeed, I didn't know what to do next. It is totally simple for me, I am totally celibate and never had any sexual drive. If I had any leaning at all it would perhaps be towards men."

When I chide him for being interested so obviously in women's bodies he

JOHN SMITH-DODSWORTH

Barry Brickell's whimsical sculptures display his talent for bold yet witty statements.

says he takes what he wants from women's bodies: their curves, breasts and buttocks. Artists have done this since prehistoric times.

Barry comments that he has always had a high degree of sensuality. "My body has always given me sensuous pleasure. But sensuality is not sexuality." A reminder to those of us who compartmentalise sex into one area of life.

John and Lynda Matthews, who have been friends and patrons of Barry's since 1980, seek out his humorous, quirky, sensuo-erotic side and they expressly commission Barry to make singular sensual pieces for them. John and Lynda have in their collection both a 'male' and 'female' terracotta sculpture, each a Henry Moore-like perfect expression of their respective sexes. A large pair of buttocks surmounted by a vase neck sits covered in moss in their garden and numerous other pieces of a suggestive nature including a teapot sporting testicles under the spout are in the Matthews' collection. Barry comments: "I like rich animated forms, not bawdy, offensive or sexy contriva."

John and Barry have spent much time joking in their own special way about erotica of various sorts and Barry would produce a particular piece for John every so often. In a letter to John accompanying a ceramic Christmas gift of an erotic nature, Barry details his modesty about producing sexually suggestive pieces and says that he is reluctant to allow the others working at the potteries to unpack these special personal pieces from the communal kiln because they may be shocked. He says "I want to get a small gas or electric kiln of my own one day just for making naughty pots to my heart's content. A wonderful little hobby for me in my 'sterile' old age. I'm not yet very good at anatomy but will no doubt improve."

Eventually John Matthews broached the idea with Barry of making an 'erotic' terracotta wood-fired mural to fill a large brick wall at the Matthews' home in Taranaki. John recalls: "Then we got involved because Barry has a love for bricks and we have these 100,000 bricks here. Barry would come and stay with us quite frequently on various adventures and we got to the concept of these erotic murals.

"We had these brick walls and we invited Barry to consider producing some works for us to go on these walls — terracotta works against terracotta bricks and he was excited about that idea and then we talked about the subject matter and we said, Well, let's have erotic works, in this case male and female forms in various so called 'love making' positions.

"Barry was pretty excited about that. But he is a self-professed virgin in all respects and really didn't know too much about how this might all come together. So we said, OK, let's start with the literature that we have. We have some books on erotic art and erotic sculpture and books on sexual relationships. And so we piled all these onto Barry. He went through these — he had the most exciting times working through the pictures. Through the pictorial exercises of these things and from that developed the various concepts about what sort of position might be adopted by a couple that were coupling!"

Barry wrote to John and Lynda (in 1985): "I thoroughly enjoyed my one night stay with you last December. The mural Eroticus is going through its gestation period and I have your books (borrowed) in a safe place. Near the site of the old abandoned Tatu state coal mine I got my dad's car stuck and, in hunting for wood to help get the car unstuck, I came across a rich, thick deposit of bog iron oxide from an old coal mine mouth, and I used the plastic bag you gave me to protect the erotic books, for gathering this lovely rich yellow sticky iron sludge! I did take the books out first and put them into a safe place."

John continues: "Away we went from there. Each time Barry sends us a drawing which gets somewhat modified depending on our mutual wishes, to the point where it is acceptable and then, of course, the final work is somewhat modified as well — it is his creation. The lovely part about it is the impossibility of the poses. The positions are somewhat beyond human possibilities and I think that is all part of the lovely scheme of the thing. From Barry's point of view they can also sexually excite one, certainly he would call us and explain with glee how sexually excited *he* was about these works. In case the works get too explicit for those who are more modest about these things, that first work on the wall does have a removable phallus. It's one you can put on and off and I understand that in the next work that is coming [the third work], from a biological point of view, there needed to be a phallus in this new work and the solution, which has a lovely humorous connotation, is this fig leaf which is removable. You can plug it on and take it off."

I have looked at two of these erotic murals and for the life of me cannot see where any phallic shapes might fit in on their twined forms. They are delightfully oriental and active, seemingly caught in a difficult but pleasurable moment of a physical encounter, rather like mating octopuses in a natural history video.

John continues: "He comes down each time and puts them up for us, but in the first work he was having a lot of difficulty. He would call us and explain, with some anguish at times, it was a sort of an excited anguish, that he was having a lot of difficulty in creating the breast of the woman in the work and he was having a good struggle to get this breast right in terms of his image that he wanted.

"That was all happily resolved and he called us one day, he was very excited, because a lady from Coromandel had come up, heard about his problem and arrived and said to Barry, This is how breasts look, and had bared herself and he was able to then incorporate her;

Eroticus mural in terracotta, 1989.

and her breasts, her bosom, is now immortalised in this work! So we have two more of those works to come and then we are going to have one more large mural which is on the other wall which won't be an erotic one, it will be some other event."

So the first 'mural eroticus' which was commissioned in 1985 was finally installed in 1989. Barry writes: "We all think the mural looks good on the brick wall. Do you think it will need some Ivan Watkins Dow moss inducer — applied discretely? Could you post me just the portion of the paper tracing of the 'radioactive' area of the mural and I will get about doing some experiments to induce fertility. The tracing will allow me to get the correct shape. Nothing in real life is easy, nor is it meant to be — eh?"

The mural is still devoid of moss masquerading as pubic hair so Barry may not have begun this proposed little garden growing exercise which would be a fittingly challenging and unusual one.

Now I have placed a number of sketches of Barry throughout his life in front of you. Many of his friends have discussed with me at length the topic of has he done it — if so with whom? Barry states that he is a virgin but even his obviously continuous 'celibacy' has been scoffed at by some friends and I have reached one conclusion: Barry has a sexuality which is expressed in his

Barry delights in creating 'naughty pots' for his own amusement.

own unique way. This expression has developed over the years and evolved into something which seems to be entirely satisfactory to him. It includes his sensual pots and other ceramics. It includes all the things Barry feels most passionate about: native forests and plants, engineering and form in art.

What he does not now and probably never has included is other people. Barry is self-sufficient sexually and harms no one with this. He should be envied rather than resented for his erotic autonomy and just allowed to get on with his life. Perhaps the discussion of this part of his life will never go away but it is well-balanced and normal for any human to not need another for their sexual needs. We are too often pushy about our own sexual preferences without allowing other people to be different and to enjoy their differences.

Barry's idiosyncrasies are a part of what has given us a superb railway, new sculptural forms and a unique and delightful individual who loves and celebrates this planet with open arms. Few of his generation have taken the environmental stance or the moral viewpoint Barry has about New Zealand and our natural resources.

Vive la différence!

CHAPTER SEVEN

THE HISTORY OF DRIVING CREEK RAILWAY

VISUALISED, DESIGNED & ENGINEERED BY BARRY BRICKELL

"Mankind has never evolved a more beautiful and environmentally benevolent instrument for heavy transport than a well-engineered narrow gauge railway."
– Barry Brickell

Throughout his life, Barry Brickell has balanced his wide and varied interests, concentrating on each interest or 'hobby' as it occurs to him. Many people have simply regarded Barry as a creative craft potter and sculptor, which he is, but equally machinery, engineering, invention and pioneering discovery are the exciting mainstays of his life and work.

So at times, when Barry has gone into engineering mode, some of the potters at DCR have neither liked nor understood the need Barry has to build in metal as well as clay; to channel energy into all the interesting ways that machines (particularly steam engines) can work. Making life easier at DCR and creating along the way a vast collection of tools, experience, innovation and invention, has been one of Barry's ideals. Because of this, the potters and residents there have benefited in many ways from Barry's expertise with machinery.

Few other potteries have such a reliable and efficient plumbing system so far from a town supply. The water is fresh from the bush clad hills and collected in an old mine shaft beside one of the streams on the property. There is available for general use heavy machinery of every kind, metal lathes, welders, clay blungers, potters' wheels, blowers for the kilns, a pug mill and brick making machine. There are electric and steam engines to run all these.

Two diesel locomotives are available to pull the wagons up the line to collect firewood for the kilns and clay to be processed into 'clay bodies' for making terracotta, stoneware and earthenware. No other pottery has the clay

(Opposite) The most spectacular engineering feature on the 3 km of track is this double-deck viaduct..

PHOTOGRAPH: JOHN SMITH-DODSWORTH

brought down from the hillside quarry pits by rail to the pug mill. The railway makes the job of transporting heavy objects around the potteries and railyard far easier than in other large potteries where wheelbarrows and brute force are required to carry the clay and pots between the raw material state and fired finished product.

Barry has always been interested in what makes things work and railways in particular have always fascinated him. When he was a student he astonished people like Dennis Hanna and Peter Tomory by taking his newly discovered LPs of train recordings to their homes to play them on their audio equipment as Barry had no stereogram of his own. Barry would sit "in raptures as a cacophony of engine noises echoed from wall to wall". Blissfully listening to the recordings of actual steam trains working: entering stations, running at certain speeds, passing over viaducts and through tunnels, ascending and descending steep grades, then later he would imitate them as he went to sleep.

He invented techniques using a ruler and sometimes a spinning wheel to assist him in making the noises more realistic. At times Barry would put on a performance of steam train noises for his friends and they were astonished by the realism and facility which he achieved. He would offer this as a new kind of musical experience.

Peter Yeates remembers: "One of Barry's evening entertainments would be to gather his railway friends, light a big coal fire and simulate the conditions of a steam locomotive and railway. He would serve 'train tea' and 'train cake' at these gatherings. He'd have the chimney blocked up and a sewing machine with sonic devices to imitate the sound of the train in various ways.

"He had a device, one of his 'fun machines', which was a big wheel attached to the wall along with the large V-belt drive off an old sewing machine with the connecting rod hanging off the belt. You could spin the big wheel on its cogs and the belt with its free hanging connecting rod would reveal to the viewer an extraordinary phenomenon: as the wheel gradually lost energy it seemed energy was lost through the rod and it would dance from side to side. The rod would perform these incredible gyrations, like a spastic orgasm; it was infectious, people would stand watching, shrieking with laughter and hugging each other watching this machine."

Barry's delight in train noises led him to set up in his earliest long drop toilet, a machine consisting of a pulley running on a V-belt wheel attached to a handle with a gourd as a sounding board. When you attended to the calls of

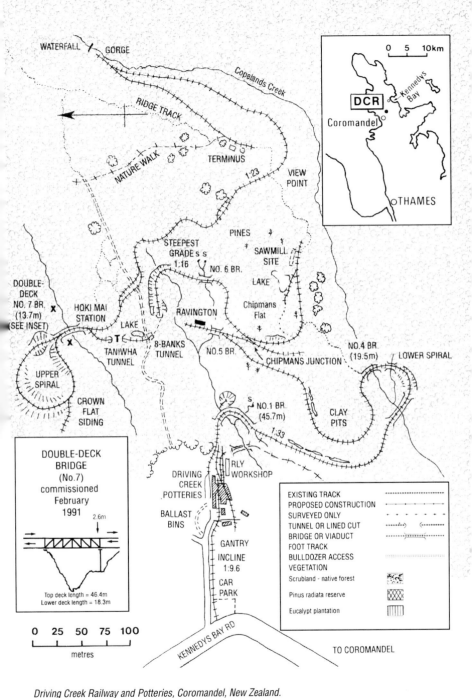

Driving Creek Railway and Potteries, Coromandel, New Zealand.

MAP: BARRY BRICKELL

nature and perhaps were bored or wished to let anyone else know you were occupied on the throne, you could turn the handle and get a perfect reproduction of a train travelling either slowly or faster and faster, depending on the speed at which you turned the handle. Children loved this contraption, which sadly no longer exists.

He also devoted a large amount of time to travelling New Zealand by rail and became fascinated with the remnants of the bush tramways, which wound through the bush and fed logs to the old steam mills in the high King Country and on the West Coast of the South Island. Barry had a number of railway enthusiast friends who would join him on some of these expeditions and this is how David Black and Merv Smith, both rail buffs from a young age, describe one journey of exploration which took place over five days in the summer of 1967.

Merv recalls: "David and I travelled to the West Coast on the 'Paper Car' which left Christchurch at 1.20 am and travelled to Greymouth to deliver the newspapers. We met Barry in Greymouth, then took the railcar to Hokitika and when we got there we hired a rental car. The man who hired us the car was quite suspicious of our intentions with the car and quite rightly so."

David remembers that he requested an older rental car but that they were given a brand new Morris 1100 for their trip. They drove to Lake Kaniere for breakfast.

Merv continues: "We pulled into the garage/tearooms and a girl took our orders. Then came my first real understanding of Barry's nature — she gave us cellophane pats of jam to go on our toast and Barry said, Excuse me? What tiny minded person thought of these? Don't you have a pot of jam? ... and she said 'Nah'. She didn't care."

David and Barry had decided that on this trip they would travel light and 'rough it.' Merv had never slept out of a bed in his life before. They drove down to Ross and looked at the Ruatapu Mill site.

Merv: "Barry said we were going down this road which said 'Road Closed' knocking hell out of the car. The reason the road was closed was because the bridge had washed out. Not put out, Barry and David rebuilt the bridge with the old pieces of wood from the original bridge which were lying scattered in the stream bed. Then Barry very, very slowly drove the car across the bridge. Down at the bottom of the road was an old timbermill. When we had finished looking at this mill we drove back up and found that the bridge had collapsed

Outside contractors were used to sandblast and repaint steelwork on No. 2 bridge, 1991.

so we rebuilt it again, then Barry very slowly drove across it and, right behind him, it collapsed once more."

The first night they slept at a camping ground and Merv was most uncomfortable as they slept on the hard ground. David and he shared a little two-man tent which collected a lot of condensation inside it. Merv only had light pyjamas, since he did not own anything designed for cold weather and mistakenly he stood up, brushed against the tent, got soaked through and lay there all night, very wet and cold in his thin sleeping bag — it was high summer but still very cold in the West Coast nights. Barry slept soundly on any surface, he would take a sleeping sheet with him and one blanket. For additional warmth he would use fern fronds and newspapers.

David adds: "We drove to Lake Brunner, right round Inchbonnie where there was still tramway equipment and an oil engine powered mill. To get it to go you had to light a fire to get the oil to vaporise. I had illegally borrowed an NZBC tape recorder and we did some sound recording, but we didn't do that much because we had a lot of trouble with it. We recorded a tape of Jimmy Gibson at Red Jacks, then we went up to his steam winch to record this thing but the tape recorder refused to go. We found a piece of copper, improvised a soldering iron, fixed the tape recorder and Merv and I did some recordings. We recorded the sound of a Dispatch logger [diesel bush loco] pulling a train across the bridge at the Rough River bush tramway. [This was the last operating bush tramway in New Zealand and lasted until the bridge washed away.] We took a lot of photographs and Merv took some 8mm film which he still has."

Merv remembers: "Barry knew everybody and I was impressed with his sense of physical place. At the back of Lake Brunner there was a pub, 'Mitchells' and across the road was a boatshed. Barry asked for a boat in the morning and we paid $5 each to sleep in an old mill house. The best thing about it was that we lit a huge fire, burning bits of the house to keep warm."

In the morning there was a solid impenetrable white fog and they were to motor across the lake to the wharf at Baynes Bay. "It looked impossible but Barry had a map. He sat in the stern with this map in his hand, steered straight into the fog and 20 minutes later we hit the old wharf dead on. Barry had never ever been there before. He picked up bits of old brake handles and other junk at Baynes Bay which had been the wharf at the timber mill — it was all piles in the water. Soon after that the sun came out. Barry was not inclined to wear good clothes and his shorts were so rotten they just fell off him so he left them where they lay. He had no underpants; he delved into his rucksack and got out another pair just as awful."

David remembers: "Barry just loves gasworks and introduced me then to this phenomenon. This passion of mine for gasworks is totally Barry's fault. On this trip we visited both the Greymouth and the Christchurch gasworks."

Barry was an early member of the NZ Railway & Locomotive Society (founded in 1944), joining 1955. He is also a founder member of the NZ Rail Preservation Society formed in 1966–67. He played a key role in the salvage and rescue of several steam engines, stationary boilers and bush locomotives.

Barry learned, along with David Black, how to repair and maintain steam boilers and at DCR he owns a 15 horsepower Dispatch boiler manufactured in Greymouth and five engines which run from the steam generated by this boiler. These engines will then operate via pulley belts several different machines: the pug mill, the blunger, the jaw crusher and the pan mill.

John Matthews, a professional engineer himself, comments about Brickell engineering and lifestyle: "We love his forms and his organic works. I trained as a mechanical engineer so I enjoy his engineering activities as well and he is very good at that. Barry has a marvellous capacity for undertaking engineering works. We were buying ceramic works in the early stages and then the steam engine [Locomorph] became our first commission and Barry needed some help with respect to an engine for his railway, so I offered to construct for him the running gear if he supplied the wheels. Then we did the axles and the frame for his grunty engine, the sort of traction engine which he pulls cargo up and down with now, clay and logs [*The Elephant*].

"So at Fitzroy Engineering — which was a company we owned at the time, a very big engineering company — we built his drive gear: the axles and the bearings and the gears and the driving system for his engine. I did that for Barry as a contribution towards helping him with getting Driving Creek underway. This was part of our involvement with Driving Creek Railway and as a

Driving Creek is a genuine working railway, as well as a tourist attraction.

consequence we got to know him further still. I just felt Barry needed help, was worthy of assistance. He is an extremely competent engineer.

"Barry is absolutely sincere, absolutely honest, he speaks his mind, he speaks his heart, and a lot of people can read him, I think, as being somewhat simple or not very clever, but actually Barry is an extremely clever person, very competent, he has got a science degree. But when you meet him none of these characteristics come out. There's the other part of him, the almost at times childlike happiness, which is what we have lost in life; this he has been able to maintain so Barry is extremely pleasant company and full of a very good spirit of humanity. "The other thing he has is his *extraordinary* energy; he is up at the crack of dawn, literally, and up the railway line to lay some more line and then comes down for breakfast and then is away again and simply works from dawn to dusk. He has this great Grand Project and he is not going to be diverted from this project at any cost.

"Barry has two major frustrations. One is that he never has enough money to achieve his ambitions quick enough. That is a well known frustration for lots of people who have high ambitions. When Barry is creating he is so ambitious. It is marvellous that he has created so much of his Grand Scheme. He also has a frustration with people mindlessly taking up his time because he has got so much to do. They come up there and he is not strong enough to push them off and get on with the job; and he needs also to be polite so he can get some money from them so he can go further with his work."

Barry began tracklaying at the Potteries in 1974 shortly after he bought the property, which was mostly covered in tall kanuka scrub and some mature radiata pine. There were some grassy paddocks and a barn on the property as well. The pottery workshop and kilns were established first and to service the potteries a short length of railway, laid to a gauge of 15 inches [381mm] was initially built to bring pine wood and yellow terracotta clay down from the hill to the pottery. The wood is sawn up and stacked to dry on wagons under cover and is used to stoke the wood-fired kilns. The clay is obtained from pits and cuttings beside the railway track and after mixing it with kaolin and river sand and processing by pugging the resulting terracotta is used for brick and tile making, garden ware and sculpture.

Not satisfied with building and running an efficient pottery utilising railway track, Barry still had in mind his Grand Scheme, a narrow gauge mountain railway climbing up into the hills behind the potteries. Elaborating on the idea which he had developed earlier as a project for his Waikawau property, that of building New Zealand's first true mountain railway, his Grand Scheme became the desire to combine conservation, engineering and art.

So Barry made a gradiometer from an old Vickers gunsight and a camera stand and began to cut survey tracks through the scrub. He spent countless hours planning, calculating grades, clambering about in the dense undergrowth and climbing trees to survey the best route for the planned railway from the potteries to the ridge top, which he had decided should be 'The Terminus'.

Barry decided that the gauge of the track would be 15 inches. This gauge allows the least amount of excavation and the tightest curves that can be negotiated while allowing human sized rather than miniaturised trains and carriages to be built.

Barry's first railway system was 10½-inch gauge which was very limited in scope. It would be impossible to get enough of the curved section rail to create the sort of railway he envisaged, carrying passengers up and down the hillside and eventually carrying the heaviest of locomotives, the steam engine Barry had always dreamed of owning since his youth.

The 15-inch gauge was new to New Zealand but is recognised internationally as 'estate gauge', the smallest practical gauge for commercial passengers and goods. Rails were not readily available for purchase, even as scrap metal,

TIM CHAMBERLAIN

Bogie unit on The Snake.

but some small sawmill and council railways were gradually being phased out around the country. Barry has a network of railway enthusiast and engineer friends who notify him of any source of old rails they may find hidden in the mines, hills and cities. He was fortunate to obtain truckloads of scrap rail from Waikato coal mines that were being closed or modernised at the time.

Because of the rugged and steep nature of the Coromandel hillside, some steep grades and sharp curves had to be laid out but the steepest grade, of 1 in 16, is located on a straight section of track through a cutting. On curved sections the grade is not steeper than 1 in 18. Many bridges had to be planned and a total of seven bridges have been built. The first of these is an engineering wonder. It begins just beyond the workshop and potteries; from there the viaduct springs immediately out into the treetops, curving gently for the first half of its 46 metre length over a deep ravine with two creeks chattering far below. Tall kanuka trees tower above and punga tree ferns brush by as the train passes through the treetops crossing the long beautiful bridge.

Much of the track and the cuttings were dug out by hand but a bulldozer was brought in to shape the massive earth embankment underneath the curve linking the two levels of the double-deck viaduct (Bridge No. 7). This viaduct is unique in that the train crosses it twice in the one journey, firstly heading north on the lower deck, negotiating a spiral, and then recrossing southbound on the upper level travelling towards Hoki Mai (Keep on Returning) Station.

From Hoki Mai Station there is a great view of the Hauraki Gulf, a picnic and barbecue area, an arboretum specialising in native shrubs and a network of bush tracks forming a fine ramble through the native kauri reafforestation project. Hoki Mai is at the end of the most spectacular 2.5 km stretch of the railway which includes two switchbacks, two tunnels and the spiral between the two viaduct levels.

The double-deck viaduct is an incredible engineering feat. First planned by Barry in 1988, the cables were swung across the ravine late that year and a temporary swingbridge built to allow access to the bridge foundation works which were largely hand built into the steep hillside. The swingbridge consisted of a series of fencing wire loops hanging from a pair of wire cables across the deep ravine with a nine inch wide board through the loops. Across this swaying plank, concrete was barrowed to be poured into the foundations.

The steel beams to construct the main span (45 feet long) of the viaduct were trucked in and the parts drilled and fitted at the DCR workshops. The span of the viaduct was prefabricated beside the workshops and temporarily bolted up so the reassembly points could be accurately marked. Then it was disassembled, and the various beams transported and reassembled as each beam was carefully swung into place with the help of a chain block and travelling pulley running on a cable above the bridge. The swingbridge was gradually demolished as the permanent beams were located and bolted into place. Designing the main span required the help of a professional engineer; he called in his friend Nelson Valiant.

Barry's native New Zealand pioneering skill was put to use in solving the problem of bridging what to most of us are simply overgrown ravines, which few of us would visualise being traversed by a railway, requiring gentle grades and wide curves to ascend this tortuous hillside. For Barry, this is the challenge, to be an unexpected pioneer, to change the course of 'progress' and create a lasting sustainable environment where heavy engineering and industry can coexist beside native forest in the best of all possible marriages.

The double-deck viaduct was finally opened on 9 February 1991. This is the announcement made by the owner at the time:

Viaduct completed. The completion of the DCR first stage of development in Coromandel was marked by a ceremony to open the double-deck viaduct. The manager of the railway, Mr Humphrey Colefax, spoke of the prosperity that this enterprise would bring to the area. Apart from irregular passenger services the main traffic on the line would be goods trains carrying milk containers, pottery clay and diesel and coal fuel.

The Railroad Tycoon Industrialist and Managing Director of the railway I.B. Brickell Esq. intimated that the main outward freight on the line would be from his potteries and that the aesthetic concern shown in the construction of the line would be reflected in the nature of the goods carried on it to all parts of New Zealand for sale and exhibition.

The viaduct was paid for largely by the output of the potteries and Barry's exhibitions, for which he continued to make ceramics throughout the railway construction, maintaining a work schedule which would be punishing for most men if only one aspect of the work done was pursued, for example the viaduct construction.

The train journey is long and satisfyingly mysterious. The rails shine in the

MECHANICAL DESCRIPTION OF *THE SNAKE*

Overview
The unit is purpose-designed for the arduous track conditions that pertain to the Driving Creek Railway; ie sharp curves (down to 7.5m radius), a ruling grade of 1 in 16 and track consisting of varying grades of second-hand rails. Gear ratios in the transmission are set to give a normal running speed of 10km/hr at 1,300 RPM from the Fordson Major 73 HP diesel engine. The DCR is an extremely scenic line and there is no need to run tourist passenger trains at higher speeds.

Mechanical Description
A four-bogie, double-articulated design was adopted, with the two articulating joints situated over the centres of the two middle or inner bogies. This will provide a very flexible yet good track holding arrangement. The two end units are well decked between the bogies with the driver's compartment arranged forward of the front bogie. The whole unit is symmetrical about the midpoint, and is fully reversible. The centre unit has straight frames which carry the engine and reverse box amidships. There is room on it for some additional fixed passenger seats.

Driver's Controls
The driver's controls will be arranged on a pedestal behind an openable windscreen designed for full forward visibility. Reversing will be done by remote control of the reversing box which is hydraulically operated. Throttle and braking will also be mounted for remote control with a key system carried by the driver for operation from either end of the train. Sanding apparatus will be direct-controlled at each end from the cab, under which the sandboxes will be situated.

Bodywork
Simple swinging mid-height doors with latches will be fitted along the train opposite the gaps between the seats. The "open air" plan for passengers is practical and essential for enjoyment of travel on the railway. It would be inconceivable to enclose passengers inside a weatherproof compartment with windows as many of the spectacular views are obtained by looking down over the viaducts. This is accomplished safely by the provision of see-through netting sides. Although some clearances along the line are tight, it is considered that suitable notices and the driver's personal warning prior to the start of every trip will ensure a maximum degree of safety.

Bogie Design Features
The cast steel wheels from A&G Price Ltd were machined here at the DCR workshop, but until the pattern-maker could add to the flange depth, the first lot of wheels had to be built-up by welding. They were then stress-relieved at 600°C in the gas-fired kiln. While one wheel was shrink-

fitted to each axle, the other was fitted with a bronze bush to run on a turned journal near the other end of the axle. Retainer rings were machined up and fitted and provision for internal lubrication of the bush from the outside was made.

Self-aligning spherical double-roller bearings were fitted into the machined horn blocks which can move slightly in their vertical guides below a pair of very stiff springs within the bogie frame. These springs are intended as shock absorbers rather than to do most of the cushioning work for the main frames. This latter is done within the pair of cross pieces or bolsters straddling the centres of the bogie frames. They consist of upper and lower channels, one fitting within the other with the main coil springing in between. This allows for a very compact design. A little lateral movement dampened with end spring pairs can take place between both bolsters to cushion the side shocks. A heavy machined pin passes up through the bolster centre to locate and provide for the articulating of the main frame of which it forms the end member.

Transmission
With sixteen wheels to drive on sharply curved track, a very flexible type of transmission had to be adopted. An hydraulic drive was seen to be the most appropriate, with either sixteen independent motors (one per wheel), or eight motors, one to the left and the other to the right pair of wheels of each bogie. NZ Hydraulics was consulted to advise on the most suitable arrangement.

Braking
A modern truck-type automatic air braking system will be fitted; the piping will be a dual circuit providing ordinary service brakes to all four bogies and an emergency air-operated spring brake operating on the two inner bogies. Dual air receivers and non-return valves will be fitted to ensure safe operation. An independent mechanical track/emergency brake will also be fitted.

A feature of the braking system will be the provision of emergency brake valves (taps) for the use by passengers with one valve being located in the centre of each passenger compartment. A compressor is fitted to the engine and the operating range for the air system will be between 80-120 lbs/sq in. Normally, the train will run down the line under engine compression as this has been found to be most satisfactory.

Endnote
The passenger train described herein is the first of its kind in NZ, and has many features found in the latest designs of modern light-rail vehicles (LRVs) overseas.

Barry Brickell, June 1992 (Abridged)

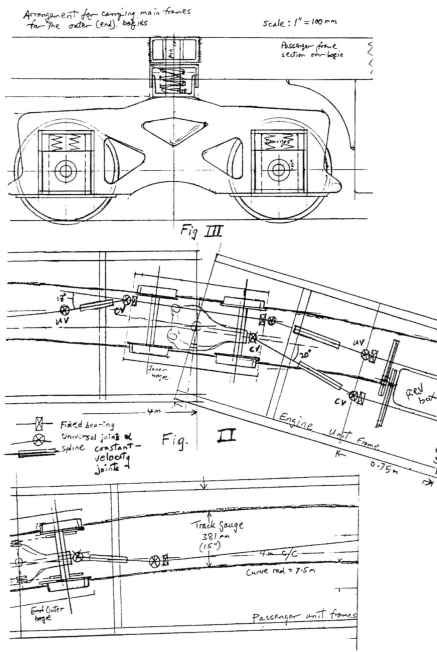

Arrangement for carrying main frames for the outer (end) bogies

Scale : 1" = 100 mm

Passenger frame section over bogie

Fig III

18°

UV

CV

Inner bogie

20°

UV

CV

REV box

4m

Engine Unit Frame

0.75 m

⊠ → Fixed bearing

⊗ → Universal joints &

⟶ spline constant-velocity joints

Fig. II

Track Gauge 381 mm (15")

4 m c/c

Curve rad = 7.5 m

End Outer bogie

Passenger unit frames

Barry Brickell's scale drawings for Snake *trainset: (Fig.II) Transmission; (Fig.III) Bogie profile.*

sun and rain curving ever on and up the hill, polished by many journeys each day. Sometimes, down below a bridge, you can glimpse a terracotta bathing beauty about to dive into a pool, or taniwhas rising out of the lake further up the line. There is a golden lion on a plinth at Hoki Mai, a half hidden waterfall pool, a dribble fountain which looks like tiers of breasts dripping algae, and glow worms in the deeper cuttings at night. Statues and terracotta sculptures of many kinds are hidden all along the journey, some becoming overgrown with the luxuriant ferns and mosses of the encroaching bush. Young kauri and rimu begin to tower over the track and the view will eventually need to be maintained if anything of the Hauraki Gulf is to be seen from the track.

Sometimes the train will take the branch line up to Chipman's Lake where a bush picnic spot and nature walks are being developed near a sawmill site. Here too there is another terracotta sunbathing beauty and a mermaid sitting on a rock overseeing the level of the lake as it rises and falls seasonally under the hot Coromandel sun and torrential rains.

The rolling stock and trains are also purpose-built at the engineering workshop at DCR. The original locomotive is a small four wheel diesel with an 8 hp Kubota engine. This, the *Diesel Mouse*, was built in 1976 by Lofty Holman, an engineer friend. The *Mouse* helped extend the railway for a considerable distance up the hill.

The second locomotive is a double-bogied shaft-driven design powered by a 65 hp Ford diesel engine commissioned in 1978. This was christened *The Elephant*. It is a modern type of the classic diesel Dispatch Logger used on the bush tramways of the King Country and it can haul the heaviest passenger and freight trains up the steep grades. Until the more recent railcars were commissioned, *The Elephant* hauled the daily passenger trips up the line. John Matthews helped Barry with the building and construction of this locomotive using his engineering company facilities to make parts of the train that were too difficult to do at DCR.

Barry eventually decided to have his railway officially inspected by an engineer so that he could be certified to carry fare-paying passengers. His cousin Derek Brickell, a civil engineer, agreed to do the inspection as required by the Public Works Act and recommend alterations to improve safety.

Derek comments about the procedure they used: "It needed a very pragmatic approach to being an inspector, because the materials Barry was using to build the viaducts were recycled beams and the like and they sometimes defied any engineering analysis — while still being vital to the railway and holding up life and limb. So we devised a technique of inspection which involved empirical load testing. We doubled the load of a group of passengers and tested the bridges for any change in the structures' stability.

"We could measure bridge performance and work along those lines. With all the carriages we looked for a pragmatic solution for all the potential hazards and improve on it. Barry's approach was totally supportive for all the safety issues and all it needed was someone to point out

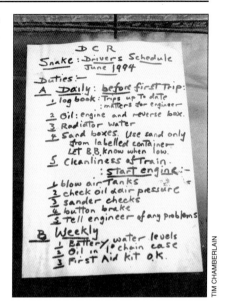

Train drivers' instructions.

details and ensure the improvements were made. Detailed reinforcing needed to be made on the bridges and a change of train type so there would be no reversing down the hill with the engine behind the train. Plus a regular maintenance programme was set up with a regularly kept log of maintenance inspections. By putting it down as a procedure this made it independent of Barry. They were mostly things he did anyway but it was made into a system."

Barry is very safety-conscious for his passengers and under his new system there have been no major problems on the steep track. Because of the necessity for switchbacks to traverse the hillside, a train with an engine at only one end would have to reverse for a part of the journey. Barry solved this potentially dangerous problem by devising, designing and building an entirely new type of articulated railcar with every wheel driven, every wheel braked, for maximum adhesion and safety on the steep grades. The engine is mounted in the centre of the railcar, with a driver's controls at each end of the car.

Throughout 1992 Barry employed an engineer (fitter and welder) to carry out his plans. Many hours of engineering drawings were made and towards the end of the year a team of people was involved in completing the train for the anticipated heavy passenger traffic of the summer holidays.

Commissioned on Christmas Eve 1992, *The Snake* has proved a successful passenger railcar after a few teething troubles. It was built to cater for tour bus loads of visitors and can seat 50 people, providing everyone with a view of the bush while the roof keeps rain showers off the passengers. This must be a record load for one articulated vehicle on a 15-inch gauge railway. Powered by a 76 hp Ford diesel engine, it is shaft-driven to all 16 wheels which are grouped into four bogie sets with the body articulation points over the inner pair of bogies and the engine carried amidships on the centre body unit. It has a driver's cab at both ends so it is fully reversible.

Then a 20-seater carriage fitted with air brakes was planned. It was designed to be towed by *The Elephant*, replacing the original carriage built by Jason (Lofty) Holman in 1986. However, it was found not to be sufficiently safe on wet rails and was converted into a motorised 20-seater railcar for lighter passenger work during cooler wet weather, using the same principle as *The Snake*: every wheel driven, every wheel braked. This small railcar, completed in 1994, is called *The Possum*. It now runs with *The Snake* during the busy summer months and will run as required during the winter months while *The Snake* has its overhaul.

Next on the drawing board is a steam locomotive. Because of forest fire risk during the summer months this could only be used in the winter or in

Early sketch for proposed DCR steam locomotive (BB, 7/11/81).

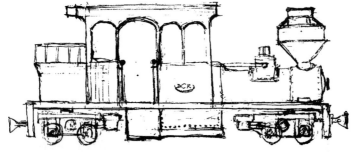

wet weather. DCR will not be complete without a steam engine. It will haul one passenger car with 20 people up the steepest grades and will have a wood-fired multi-tubular boiler with cylinders 4x6 inches [115x152mm]. Barry assures me that the steam loco will be used for ceremonial occasions only. Virtually all the parts are in the workshop. The decision on its construction may be left until the Terminus is complete.

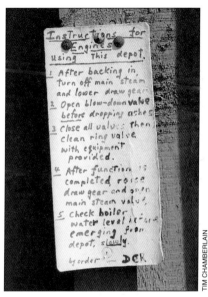

Instructions placed at entrance to public toilets.

At Driving Creek there is also a battery electric maintenance and inspection vehicle with modern thyrosistor controlled motors. Particular attention is paid to braking so all trains and wagons are fitted with automatic air braking for passenger work and screw-down brakes on work wagons.

I look forward to celebrating with Barry and all the workers, friends and supporters who have helped over the last 20 years to construct this railway when the last line is laid at Driving Creek Railway. We will look down at the fabulous view of the islands and coastline of the Hauraki Gulf outlined in black and silver, while around us kauri, rimu and other native seedlings are already beginning to show through the kanuka scrub.

The natural energy of the place affects everyone who comes here. It feels good to be at this place, great to be alive. Each trip on the Driving Creek Railway will be a celebration of the values Barry Brickell has worked so hard for throughout his life.

Of one thing I am certain: that Barry will not rest on his laurels for long and soon one of his new projects will be keeping him busier than ever.

CHAPTER EIGHT

DRIVING CREEK TODAY

"Indeed I am perhaps reinventing the industrial revolution, but with a conservational rather than an exploitive twist."
                                                                    – Barry Brickell

November 1994

This morning Barry Brickell is busy discussing catering arrangements for the summer with a man who turns out to be a complete stranger. The discussions are inconclusive. He is too busy to talk to me yet.

Barry sold two terracotta sculptures over Labour Weekend and delivered these to Auckland yesterday in the ancient buff-coloured VW with the passenger seat removed to make room for his large sculptures, which are over a metre in height. He brought two sculptures back from Auckland to put into the sculpture garden to replace the sold ones. So he wasn't here when I called to interview him yesterday, although we had discussed last week that I would be driving over from Auckland to begin talking about the book project. Instead I interviewed his mother, Shirley Brickell.

Today he is too busy until 1pm to sit down to be interviewed so together we clean off a tiny table in the clay-dusty library and I begin to go through the personal papers in two folders he has given me. Someone else has sorted these out and filed them for Barry.

As I am working through his papers he comes up the stairs and says to me "There are so many people, I will take the railcar up as well." This is interesting; a huge tour of children and adults from Hong Kong has arrived, and subsequently both trains head up the hill, passing each other on the switchbacks. Barry drives the railcar *Possum* and his paid driver Beran Whitcombe, the articulated train, *The Snake*.

The library is next to Barry's simple bedroom on the upper floor. Art works gifted to him adorn the walls, his clothes lie in simple abandon on a large dark stained table against one wall. The single unmade bed seems that of a

NOT THE *THING* BUT *HOW*

A Personal Code

This statement has become a code which I use to solve or evaluate the indecisions and puzzles that confront me in life. Over the years, I have not been able to improve upon it and indeed, I have found it to be wonderfully watertight as a basis for rational thinking.

To take an example, let us consider say gold mining. This is a controversial issue here in Coromandel, between business interests and conservationists (if such a species exists). I say that the issue then (ie the thing) is not gold mining but the manner (the how) in which it is done. As with any other activity, gold mining may be done well or badly, depending on the criteria that the individuals, singularly or collectively, choose to decide upon.

Then there is, for instance, the controversial matter of art *versus* craft, which argument has pervaded discussion between artists, craftspeople and lookers-on for years. Based on my code, I can then say: Art is to Craft as How is to Thing. The rationale here is the fact of the unique nature of each human individual as born, being a factor in the creation of a work of art. Thus, firstly we each have our own way of doing the same thing. Secondly, when in front of an audience (one or more other people), if we do it with appropriate eloquence and expression and innocence, we then create a "work of art". In consideration of this, the medium (thing) is not limited and so the rule is universal. The craft aspect is limited to the practice. Crudely put then, the way of the crafting is the potential for art.

Some people have suggested that I substitute the word Why for How in my code statement. This represents a failure to understand its real meaning. This would tilt it in the direction of irrationality, faith, or at worst, religion, which are separate issues.

I like to think that I can lend a strong sense of optimism for modern "Western-type" humanity through the reassurance of individual spirit in the face of so much media negative influence. It seems that how to provide fulfilment (the thing) in so many young human lives remains a question of enormous importance. Perhaps as a concluding clout, I can end with the statement: There is no such thing as teaching; only the how of learning. Now then, consider the rank stupidity of the idea of the "Art School".

– *Barry Brickell, November 1995*

refugee and matches that in his other earlier 'temporary' bedroom on the upper level (now the office).

Looking out the window which is liberally spattered with clay, I see that Barry's studio is reached via a series of planks a foot wide, which span the gap over the platform between the upper verandah roof of the main building outside Barry's bedroom and his upper level studio. You can stand there on the plank and observe the passengers and potters from above. Today down below me, James McDougal, one of the resident potters, is throwing magnificent urns and jars on the potter's wheel to the delight of the visitors. He is superb to watch.

TIM CHAMBERLAIN

Wailin Elliott is a neighbour, close friend and artistic collaborator of Barry's. Her distinctive 'mermicles' can be found in the most suprising places at Driving Creek, including aboard HMS Auful *at right.*

Barry spends a lot of his time in his studio facing the sun on a level above the platform. Originally he had the bulldozer cut out a two level area for Driving Creek Potteries and up here are the now subsidiary railyard for the small locomotives *Diesel Mouse* and *The Elephant*, which transport clay, timber, bricks and other building materials up the line; the mobile rail workshop which he tows up the line; and the row of sheds that are now Barry's office and studio.

Outside his studio sits his home-made potter's wheel, of very simple design and lacking a tray to catch water or clay scraps. He built this wheel in 1962 and Bernard Leach threw the very first pot on it. Over all this tower several tall manuka trees which drop their black rain of leaves and sticks continually over the roof and everything below.

In the studio the only concession to comfort is the home-made pot belly stove. He may light this on cold days. There is a chipboard tabletop balanced on a box and a beer crate and staple box set with 'cushing irons' to sit on.

Back in the library the books are stacked everywhere and covered in clay dust. Wailin Elliott has her wheel and work area four feet away from the

TIM CHAMBERLAIN

HMS Auful, *a Brickell-Elliott work, was created for a Coromandel anti-mining exhibition. BB: "The story behind it is quite complex and usually falls on blind eyes and deaf ears. What is it saying?"*

books and down a short passage across the landing is the large light room James is using as his indoor studio. About half the books are Helen Mason's and half are Barry Brickell's. They are both voracious readers.

There is a virtually complete collection of *NZ Potter* magazine (Helen was editor of the magazine for the first nine years). This being the home of potters, you would expect there to be many books featuring international ceramics and techniques and these are here in abundance, but there are also books on religion (some of them in foreign languages), art in many forms, philosophy, books about architecture and many novels with New Zealand writers featuring strongly.

Parts of this building were built from the Brickell family home demolished in Devonport in the 1970s. Rough unfinished kauri timber. The long straight old floorboards are still beautiful under the clay and dust. Spiderwebs decorate the timber window frames. One window pane is decorated with a stencilled cross of clay slip spattered over the shape centred on a slide frame stuck to the window. Outside on the verandah roof, pots 'from the collection', some broken and some whole, lie in abandon 'being kept clean by the rain'. The bees from the hives up on the hill come here to drink from the pots which are full of rainwater, rotting leaves and flowers from the overhanging bush.

Below this upper storey is a huge storage and drying area for the potteries and the engineer's kitchen with coffee, tea, filthy electric jug and ancient fridge. There is a locked secret room lit by a single dust-covered light bulb called 'the archive' full of works of art collected by Barry and Helen from visiting potters, a testimony to the superb pottery made in New Zealand over the years. This archive is not on display because there are no facilities to keep the pots secure. Many are labelled and dated, though, thanks to Helen's hard work.

I am told, disapprovingly by some, that the 'community' philosophy at Driving Creek Railway has changed to the tourist business 'train running for money' sort of outlook. I cannot see this as a bad thing, simply evidence of the eventual commercial success of one man's eccentric dream, just in time for him to earn money from it to keep him alive as he gets older. Few of his community would stick around to care for him if he needed it without payment and he knows this.

The change of emphasis certainly modifies the character of DCR from the earlier impressions given to me of its being a typical Coromandel community, a model which Barry has never pretended it was. Now it has a more commercial focus on tourism where the train always runs if there are eight or more people to get on it.

Some have even complained to me that it is getting more and more like a railway station every day. "But it *is* a railway station," I reply. "The rails go right down to the road, past the kitchen and pottery shop and lead in the opposite direction up the hill into the bush. The arched roof and banner pronounce it to be a station and platform and there is the ticket office. You cannot mistake DCR for anything else *other* than a railway station."

Every day more people come to ride on the train and gaze astonished at the incredible old machines Barry has installed at DCR. Machines essential to pottery and engineering which most people never get to see. Stationary steam engines, pug mills, crushers, boilers and the engineering shop, which visitors are not encouraged to visit, has a large metal lathe and contains a bewildering assortment of metal, machines and hand tools stacked in abandon like sheaves of metallic wheat.

Faced with this railway and engineering focus, those seeking a 'spiritual life' here had best borrow a few books from the library, blow off the clay dust and walk up into the regenerating bush to set up camp by Chipman's Lake where the terracotta bathing beauty and the mermaid will watch over their contemplations. Or, like Barry, they can dig for their salvation, working physically for the sheer satisfaction of it.

We could speculate that if Barry's railway was not such an enormously expensive hobby he could have been very well off by now. The railway has now reached a stage of development where it will afford Barry an income from the one thing which has always cost him money until recently. In the past he has put almost every cent of spare money into the railway: the Grand

Resident potter Rhys Hill demonstrates technique to a visitor.

Scheme, maintaining the pottery's machinery and planting trees. He spends virtually nothing on himself.

He has no television, although he has a tiny portable transistor radio, an ancient stereo and three telephones to enable the numerous enquiries about the railway to be answered. The refrigerator and washing machine are basic and functional, shared by the other residents at DCR. He uses an old Volkswagen car that was given to him some years ago by Helen Mason.

Later I wait to talk with Barry, sitting on the dubious comfort of a staple box in his studio. "I have a stamp," Barry explains, "which simply says 'UNSATISFACTORY'. I put it on the bottom of letters I don't like and send them back. If I use it on the bottom of official letters and send them back it takes the bureaucrats ages to figure out what it means and get back to me!" He laughs uproariously and infectiously. Then he arranges on the phone for oil filters for the train engine; digs up some terracotta clay from his private store and wedges it up to begin making another ceramic hand-built terracotta sculpture on the metal turntable near the wobbly sliding door which once was mostly glass and is now mostly boarded up.

He sits on a cushion on a beer crate in front of the turntable. Eventually I get a cushion for my staple box too. As I sit crouched on the box with a clay ingrained chipboard tabletop resting on my knees, there is a huge voluted sculptural form rising to tower five feet above me on my left. It is as tall as I am and is slowly drying before firing.

The chooks cluck in the background. Barry finds their eggs where they lay them in the blackberries and under the chook house. He reaches into a lidded jar, bringing out a raisin bun which he breaks in half with his clay-encrusted hands and throws half out to the hen that is wandering perilously close to the neighbour's fence where it is not allowed to go. Immediately the clucks change almost to purrs of delight at such food and Barry is equally pleased.

He sits down to model the base of the new sculpture. He is an odd-looking individual, his feet encased in his favourite 'sandlars' or 'sandaling irons'. There is another pair of these hideous grey/brown plastic sandals under the table. Barry's feet are perpetually muddied, cracked and battered from year after year of all-weather toil and lack of care. Very organic feet. He wears simple drill pants, once dark blue but now covered in a mixture of clay and oil, rolled up almost to the knee and above these a simple deep burgundy pink T-shirt. The colour suits him well.

His body is brown, bony and muscular, well veined. Barry strikes me as a unique individual rather than as a man: he is curiously clumsy and gauche yet you sense a real solid unchanging simplicity and well-meaning attitude in his nature. He has all the charm of an old iron bedstead which has not yet outlived its usefulness. This sturdy frame has found itself capable of expressing thoughts, feelings, ideas and even sexuality with all its fascination, yet the physical needs and emotions were never there for an active sexuality shared with another person to take place.

His face is mobile and often full of beauty as he speaks of philosophy and higher things, or problems with the brakes on *The Snake*. His hands are busy, with a by now unconscious skill, rolling and shaping the terracotta clay into a solid circular base for the forthcoming sculpture.

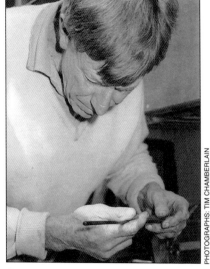

PHOTOGRAPHS: TIM CHAMBERLAIN

Barry checking train's oil level, and...

The studio is glued together with spider webs, the window is opaque with clay and webs from years gone past but still Barry uses it to peer out, counting passengers on the train and checking the departure and arrival times like a Victorian stationmaster.

Barry makes us tea with an immersion heating element in a battered, lidless burgundy red stoneware teapot, pouring out milk from a cream bottle that is sitting uncovered and half full on the bench top. We each eat a piece of the delicious birthday cake his mother made him. We drink out of his DCR mugs and eat clay with the cake like all real potters. A pot of Lanoline sits on the bench for application when the clay has dried his skin too much. A battered gritty portable typewriter rests among sheaves of papers on the drying shelves. Everything, everything is covered in clay and clay dust.

He promises we shall now 'begin to absentrate' (semi-concentrate) and we talk — not closely to the topic but ranging over many subjects and including many of the things I need to know — the building of DCR on this site, conservation, art, people we have known. He steadily builds up the thick sausages of clay he rolls into a cylinder with sigmoid ripples decorating the lower edge. Barry does not like to sit still doing nothing while talking, but while he is coiling at least he is in one spot so I can take notes or record his voice.

The Snake roars up the hill with another load of passengers. Barry goes to

find some paper to lay under the sculpture to prevent its sticking to the metal turntable and complains that all he can find is *The Listener* which he hates now because it "has faces leering out of it all year round and doesn't even burn well now, it is so full of chemicals."

Under the grimy window, postcards snuggle together gritted by clay dust and faded with age. The new ones glow like fresh glass in a grubby window. All the windows here allow only opaque light through; those which give the best light are broken. The portable phone

...cleaning windscreen prior to departure.

sits in a cup on the shelf. Occasionally when it rings Barry will answer it, moving outside for better reception.

January 1995

I have arrived at DCR on a perfect summer night accompanied by my 11-year-old daughter Ruth. The railway carriage we will sleep in has recently been inhabited by Romilly Brickell, and it shows in the improvements: soap in a dish of Helen Mason's, a fresh smell, a broken piece of an ancient bevelled mirror balanced on a small bamboo stool on the sink bench, children's playtools and pencils in the outer room which also has stacked in it several sleeping bags and a tent. Only occasionally does the floor get swept in the carriage. When the doors are open leaves blow in and wetas and stick insects crawl about on the walls and floor.

Barry was actually awake when we arrived, although it was after 10 pm. I am surprised. He insists on lighting us to the railway carriage and I assure him we shall be totally OK until the morning, that we have everything we need and that he is free to go to bed.

I suggest putting the food I brought with me into the fridge but he says his sister has filled it with food. This I shall have to see! The refrigerator here at DCR is rather like that at a student flat — extremely variable in the contents and usually sparsely furnished indeed.

Barry has retired to bed and I see the light on at the far end of the building where he sleeps. The night air is cool and extremely peaceful. Even the stars seem closer and brighter than before. We go to sleep exhausted after a hot day of travelling.

We are up out of bed at 7.30am. There doesn't seem to be a water shortage here compared with Auckland or Northland. Driving Creek obviously keeps flowing vigorously all year round but we don't know when it will rain again so no wastage. There is a total fire ban in the Coromandel and all cigarettes must be put out carefully. No one at DCR is a smoker. I asked Barry if he was a smoker ever and he said no, that he tried smoking once and it made him feel sick so he didn't try it again.

I shower with my daughter, catching the spare water in a bucket and watering the orchids and native plants in the planters outside. I offer to sweep out *The Snake* and get dirty doing this. Then I sweep the platform, washing off the patterned tiles on the dusty platform floor. Barry is oiling and checking the train before the first ride of the day and asks me if I can fix him some lunch as he is often so busy he doesn't have time to get any lunch himself. I will fire up the 'hottie' as he calls the gas cooker and create something out of the leftovers in the fridge for him.

Everything seems immensely tidy at Driving Creek Railway — the grass cut and tidied, a woman's touch everywhere, vases of flowers, pots reorganised. James is throwing pots out in the shed beside the separate ticket office which is now in use again for the summer instead of the shop. The trains will run all day every hour from 10.30am until 5pm. Barry and Beran will share the driving duty and take both trains if enough people arrive. I make lunch for Barry but he's off again, driving the third train of the day, relieving Beran who eats his sandwiches and serves in the shop.

Christine sells the tickets and answers the phone, Denise works in the Tram selling knitwear and spun wool, James throws pots and has children decorating small glazed bowls and candlesticks with low temperature glazes. One glaze is labelled with a question mark; it may turn out pink, spotted or disappear on the pot altogether. The copper is the best, causing a gorgeous luminous metallic gold and shiny copper sheen to appear on the surface of the glazed pot. All these activities are happening throughout this summer at DCR while the trains are travelling up and down the line. Everyone is friendly, busy and happy about the place. Beran takes Ruth off on a ride up the line on the first train. She wants to glaze and fire pots with James, buy comb honey and more pots.

A luxury minibus arrives with a wealthy family of six from Argentina. They want a free souvenir of no value from the railway so Barry hurries with them to get an item from the workshop. He is devoted to the railway and enjoys the tourist trade. He is thrilled deeply that at last his lifelong hobby is making him money. Barry considers it a high risk investment though, perhaps not fully appreciating its appeal to travel agents who are now sending coach loads of tourists to DCR to experience his living, working attraction of the railway and potteries. Visitors can ride the trains into the regenerating native bush, learn about steam and pottery, and take home a permanent reminder of their visit from the pottery gift shop. People will go far just to look at static trains and museums, and here in Coromandel is the vibrant, ever changing, functioning, exciting product of one man's imagination, made operational by the people he has gathered around him.

Barry usually wakes early and writes letters to his friends or maybe reads, from 4 to 6am when his radio springs into life, then he rises and walks up the track to do an hour or two of railway construction or maintenance. To be alone, walking in the bush is his great joy. After walking and working in his kingdom Barry returns regularly down the track at 8am. After this is breakfast which Barry calls 'concrete': a huge bowl of muesli and milk, Weetbix, honey-comb and fresh or cooked fruit.

Then the train must be maintained and swept, refuelled and checked for safety as the first trip leaves at 10.30am sharp. The phone often rings continuously and Barry is interrupted by visitors, the potters or engineers who work here needing one thing or another. Often perfect strangers will take up an immense amount of Barry's day expecting to chat with him, since they seem to have nothing else to do. Barry would rather be taking more ballast up the line, having his lunch, adding more coils to another sculpture or helping the engineers with their latest project.

In the summer trains run frequently and Barry will drive every second one. The trips with him are the best, as he is witty and fun, informative and entertaining all at once. Often he will pretend that the train has a flat tyre as he puts on the air brakes and they hiss loudly. I have seen him drive up and down the line all day and be as fresh as a daisy for each new journey and group of travellers. He is superb with people in groups, especially since he has a captive audience.

At 5pm is the last train and the station at DCR is filled with late afternoon sunlight. Barry will disappear up into his forest again to be alone until he feels like coming down for dinner. If anyone is still present at the dinner table he may gradually begin to elucidate his philosophy on one thing or another. The history of majolica glazes or why he is against screens, as in monitor screens, or the 'how' to use the new public address system fitted to *The Snake* which must be used sensitively.

Once fed, Barry will fall asleep, often at the table with his feet up in the middle of a conversation. He has done this for years. Every Sunday he has dinner with his mother and father and snoozes there afterwards as his mother will tolerantly complain. As they age, both father and son have improved their understanding of each other and now Barry visits his parents every day.

His bedtime is early and varies from 10.30 in summer to 8.30 in winter. Once I begin to live at DCR I find myself fitting more and more into Barry's routine, relaxing and unwinding on this wonderful hillside which seems to be a world of its own, far removed from the harried denizens of Auckland across the Hauraki Gulf. The top of the arboretum here is a great place from which to view distant Auckland. This is as close as I need get to that metropolis.

At DCR the place where the influence of visitors can most be felt is in the communal kitchen, a place magnificently constructed out of unfinished rough sawn kauri planks which were salvaged from old buildings pulled down in the 1970s. The doors and windows are all recycled too and give it a charm all of its own. The building could be 100 years old instead of 20. Built largely by the young potters at DCP in the mid-1970s, it is dark and often a bit dingy and mellow. The windows are, like all the windows here, rarely cleaned and easily dirtied. The floor was once beautifully varnished plywood sheets; now the varnish is worn off leaving a patina rather resembling that of a swept earth floor. The table is an enormous hand-adzed plank of kauri resting on elephant legs of natural branches. Two church pews provide the 'sitting tools' and someone has thoughtfully provided long cushions to add comfort to the hard wooden pews.

The windows along the kitchen bench give a good light there but the rest of the kitchen is immersed in a cool gloom, within which can dimly be glimpsed the glow of beautiful earthenware and stoneware bowls and platters, tall lidded storage jars in vague shades of brown and green, a wonderful collection of valued paintings and the glow of more kauri and stained glass.

The cups, all gifts or seconds made by different potters who have worked here over the years, hang in bright, chipped, well used abandon from nails hammered into the rafters above your head as you stand at the sink to make a cup of tea.

I decide to cook up some of the huge quantity of soy beans that Barry bought for DCR some years ago in the belief that they were good for him, not realising until too late just what a fag they are to cook. There are several large Brickell storage jars of them in the kitchen. I soak the white beans in hot water, then rinse the moths out and soak them in cold water for over 24 hours before simmering them on the stove all day and they still refuse to soften much beyond a plastic 'al dente' body. They taste acceptable with the addition of lots of tomatoes and herbs fresh from Helen's garden. Tonight there are seven people for dinner so I make an Austrian apple cake and rice pudding. Barry found a whole nest of good eggs underneath the hen house this morning so I put a double yolker into the cake.

Barry came in at about 6pm and asked what time should he appear. I said that I would have tea ready at around 7pm, that not being too late for Helen and Rodger, Ruth and I, cousin Louisa and partner Bob.

"That is far too early for me," he exclaimed, so I said that whenever he should feel like arriving for dinner that some would be left ready for him. He then left for Hoki Mai and the company of his tiny transistor radio so he could listen to the news and Radio Pacific. Taking up into the bush the dry red wine he loves, while in the cooler evening he can get more work done on the railway, working up a good appetite. The dry red has been constantly there since Barry's teenage years and is his regular evening aperitif combining relaxation and work.

We all ate our dinner together and put aside the equivalent of four helpings of refried soy beans, salad and potatoes, a large chunk of creamy rice pudding and two big slices of cake. Barry came in at about 9pm, half an hour before his usual bedtime and ate all the beans and vegetables. He didn't have enough room after that mammoth meal for the cake or rice so I urged him to put aside the desserts for his consumption later and they disappeared into his secret stash.

We were all fascinated because tonight Barry brought out from his room his medieval majolica tiles which he had collected from Spain. We washed the clay and dust off to look at them. They had the appearance of hastily done but rather beautiful blue paisley style designs on a white background. The clay base was earthenware and the white slip and glaze achieved is supposed to challenge in quality and beauty the best celadon glaze over porcelain, but I couldn't see the value in it myself. More fascinating was the fact that medieval craftsmen were achieving sophisticated glaze recipes which are now lost. We discuss the uses of baking powder, cream of tartar and potassium tartarate, which is an ancient glaze ingredient obtained from scraping vintners' barrels. Since many guests were present and Romilly walked up to join us, an animated discussion ensued.

In the past this kitchen has been full of people and light, burning candles and laughter, wine drinking parties and songs, clay and soot covered exhausted sweaty bodies and some lonely desperate souls seeking comfort. The furniture is comfortable and well worn and at least we don't get to sit on beer crates here. The walls are covered in beautiful unusual modern works of art, many gifted by the artists to Barry, the logs that frame the fireplace are worn and polished to a fine patina by the many arms and hands that have leant there warming beside the fire in after dinner conversation and argument. When the move was made to the present Driving Creek property, Barry had a policy of feeding and watering and accommodating young people, potters, artists, anyone who wanted to come and live here in the huts, provided they did half a day's work helping to build the place into his dream and a half day's work potting for themselves.

Solely self-motivated, Barry has not hesitated to use whatever help has come to hand to make his dream real. Many have resented his single-mindedness, about the railway, his coiled terracotta work, his brick making, about using the land's own resources that are under his feet, about bartering goods for services rendered, resenting too his reluctance to set an example, to be a guru, to lead and bless and sleep with the people.

Barry has never been a leader. He sets his own individual pace on a path few of us will ever travel and we can admire this without resentment once we can see that he did not ask us to come and worship at his feet. He does not demand more than a fair day's work from anyone, work for which he sets the example and leads the tireless pace every day.

He works far harder than most people and far longer every day. There are few days taken off from digging 'up the line'; few days when he does not think about DCR and his Great Scheme to the exclusion of everything else. He looks forward to lots of writing and painting in his old age, although I am not sure just how old Barry will have to be before he considers himself 'old'.

Barry is a man visibly working himself to death. This is furthest from the vision and tradition of the commune guru that anyone can get. Yet there are many who are disillusioned with Barry for this very reason. They wanted leadership and free love, drop out days and teaching, drugs, free food and beds, sex and rock and roll.

None of these have ever been available at DCR unless the resident visitors created this environment themselves.

The biggest effect that DCR has had upon the 'New Age' is in the area of conservation, particularly of native trees and plants. Early on, having studied the history of the Coromandel, Barry made the decision that native trees, particularly kauri, were the plants best suited to growing on the peninsula. This is an effort to restore the kauri forest logged and burned off in the last

150 years. He created a garden of native plants in the 1960s at the first Driving Creek Railway and then took on the mammoth task of planting out in native trees the 60 steep acres of scrub land which comprise DCR. This is an ongoing task which is important to give the railway a natural New Zealand environment through which to travel.

Upon Barry's eventual death the bulk of his land will pass into the stewardship of the QE II National Trust. This will, in effect, add to the conservation estate which forms the eastern boundaries of DCR.

In fact Barry Brickell was into trees and conservation of our natural heritage as a result of his natural inclinations and his botanical studies at the University of Auckland well before most New Zealanders had finished thinking of anything other than strip mining our islands. Only relatively recently and in a few parts of this country has it become fashionable to plant native species or indeed trees of any type except pinus radiata.

Many seekers after truth have found an example of singular power here at DCR and many have gone away unfulfilled, expectations dashed by those 'unreasonable' attitudes held by Barry where he will neither deviate nor be distracted from his Grand Scheme in hand.

* * * *

Helen Brown once wrote about Barry Brickell that he had 'sorted out life by giving it all away'. She suggested that "There are many ways of leading a successful life. One of them is to leave some corner of the earth in a better state than it was before."

This is what I see Barry Brickell has done and is doing. Gifting us all with the improvements of his newly planted native forest, his sensual terracotta sculptures and pots. With the example of his gentle, generous, unassuming jovial approach to people. With his ostentatious celibacy more openly spoken of and celebrated in one way or another than if he were in a relationship of any kind.

Finest of all, his Driving Creek Railway, a bush tramway which is reversing history by assisting the planting of forest, rather than destroying it. We must all take a part in continuing to maintain and improve this unique construction to ensure it will remain for future generations to enjoy.

Barry Brickell has lived his life as himself, often ragged, barefoot, a naturally occurring Franciscan monk. Only rarely trying to reproduce social mores for the benefit of his family or, more recently, tourists. He has harmed no one purposely with his honesty and straightforward personality. If we could all follow ourselves as truly and still say the same about our lives, how different life could be.

On another level, Barry has contributed immensely to the lives of many people. He has given them an uninterrupted space in which to develop their creativity and at the same time encouraged them to become aware of the country in which we live.

Peter Tomory, a former director of Auckland City Art Gallery, sums up his ideas about Barry Brickell and his art in this way: "Barry was developing an aesthetic which William Morris would have recognised. Basically 'medieval' as conceived from a highly industrialised age, it spurned all stylistic characteristics which could be defined as sophisticated.

"Barry as I remember him was always cheerful and, like any dedicated artist was self-confident and knew exactly what he wanted to do. He was very forthright and always interesting to talk to. One quirk of his is that I don't think he ever forgot a single thing he ever made, so that when he visited friends he would often pick up a piece he had sold maybe a couple of years before, admire it and demand to have it back! When refused he was often quite put out by this apparent lack of gratitude!

"Others who spent longer periods in Barry's company often spoke of him being 'difficult', but original artists aren't put into the world to grace society and by the nature of their gift can be offhand and unkind and selfish. It is what they create that matters and no saint ever made a work of art."

"I am not a teacher but an individual who likes to think and do as he pleases."
– Barry Brickell

APPENDIX 1

CHRONOLOGY

Barry's father Maurice Brickell qualified both in engineering and meteorology and worked as a meteorologist for the New Zealand Meteorological Service. Shirley Wooler married Maurice Brickell on 26 May 1934.

She is a journalist and worked for the *Auckland Star*, *New Zealand Herald*, *Hauraki Herald* and the *Thames Star* at various times during her career.

Ian Barry Brickell is born 26 October 1935 in New Plymouth.

Soon afterwards the family moves to Auckland and the remaining three of their four children are born in Auckland.

On 17 May 1936 the Brickells are living at 12 Glenalmond Road, Mt Eden and little Barry is enrolled on the Cradle Roll of the church school of St Andrews Anglican Church. Then the family moves to Pukeora Avenue, Remuera. Fifteen months after Barry, his sister Andrea Lyndsay is born.

1942 Maurice and Shirley buy a big old kauri villa at No.1 Tui Street, Devonport. Three months after the birth of their second son Gavin, Maurice is drafted into the war, serving as a meteorologist and is away for three years with the airforce.

1945 Shirley Brickell is a founding member of the first playcentre in Devonport in 1945. It was founded for the benefit of the wives of military personnel who were away on war service. "Many of the women lived in rather squalid naval base flats which were built like tenements. Their husbands would be away for two or three years at a time." Romilly Brickell is born; she is 13 years younger than Barry.

As a child Barry Brickell is intensely curious about the world around him and obsessed with fires and the combustion of different materials. Trams, trains, machines and how things work. Earth, clay and plants (native plants especially). He explores his environment widely, mostly alone. He attends St Anne's kindergarten, Devonport Primary School and then Vauxhall Primary School where he has his first experiences using clay.

1949 Barry attends Takapuna Grammar School, Form 3 General (moving up the following year to 4A, then 5B & 6A for his two final years). He experiments continuously with fire and collects at the local dump.

1950 Barry is in the fourth form at Takapuna Grammar School. He meets Len Castle; they begin to work together building and firing kilns and testing the clays around Auckland. At high school Barry is involved in athletics and harriers, is editor of the school calendar and laboratory assistant. He hates cadets and team sports. Barry is co-founder of New Zealand's first pottery society, The North Shore Society of Potters.

1951 In the School Certificate examinations Barry's marks are 50 in English; 48 for French; 19 for Arithmetic, 7 for Algebra; 26 for Geometry and Trig; 73 for Chemistry and 62 for General Science.

1952 In the University Entrance Examination Barry gains an accredited A pass in English, Mathematics, Physics and Chemistry. (He notes the absurdity of the exam-based system.)

Barry's first commissions come from Anthony Alpers who wants some wine cups and Rex Fairburn commissions some of Barry's coffee mugs: "God knows where he got the money from."

1953 Higher School Certificate is awarded to Barry. He is a pupil of above average ability. The principal said about him: "I have a good opinion of Barry Brickell, who has an alert and original mind (special hobbies are pottery and music). I regard him as a boy of sound character, high intelligence and pleasant nature."

1955 Barry spends a year working with the Forest Service on the Coromandel Peninsula at Tairua learning practical silviculture. Barry is included in the Auckland Society of Arts (A.S.A.) Prints, Drawings and Craft exhibition 1955. He travels to the South Island with Terry Barrow and Len Castle and meets Catherine Philips. Barry joins the NZ Railway & Locomotive Society.

1956 Barry is part-time student, and employed in the office of the Forest Service on a bursary. The family celebrate his 21st birthday at Devonport sadly because Barry missed some of his examinations. Barry resigns from the Forest Service. In order to continue his studies in 1957 Barry works as a bricklayer at Kinleith. He meets Wailin Hing and they become friends.

1957 Barry is introduced to Theo Schoon by Len Castle. He exhibits again at the A.S.A. Art and Craft exhibition. He attends Colin McCahon's Thursday night painting classes at Auckland City Art Gallery. In November Barry exhibits at the first NZ Studio Potters (NZSP) Exhibition, Otago Museum. Barry's sculptural forms are exhibited as a trio with Louise Henderson and Phil Slight (who was the art teacher at Westlake Boys' High) at Auckland City Art Gallery (ACAG).

1958 Barry is living at No 7 Suiter Street, Newmarket, where he shares the old cottage with sculptor John Kingston. Exhibits at NZSP second exhibition at the Architectural Centre Wellington October 1958. Tutors with Len Castle at the ninth Adult Education Art and Design school. Barry exhibits salt glazed coiled forms with painters Tim Garrity, Trevor Moffat, Hamish Keith and Peter Tennent at ACAG.

1959 October: Barry's work is in the NZSP third exhibition, McLean Park, Napier. Theo Schoon, Len Castle, Hamish Keith and Barry all search Auckland looking for suitable clays. Catherine Philips gives the Sherry Creek cottage, 50 miles south of

Nelson, to Barry. He exhibits his first coiled forms at New Vision, a craft gallery in Queen Street, Auckland.

1960 Barry gains a science degree, majoring in botany and geology, at the University of Auckland on a Post-primary Teachers' Bursary. The Auckland City Art Gallery purchases from Barry 12 salt glazed pots at £2 each. Barry's address given as 72 West Street Newton, Auckland on 7.9.1960. NZSP fourth exhibition ACAG October/November 1960.

Jim Allen commissions Barry to build an oil-fired drip-feed kiln at Kelston High School. It is completed and used and later banned from the school as a fire risk, setting a departmental precedent for future school kilns.

Barry selects Taumarunui and Taipa high schools for his training college sections. He spends three weeks teaching at Taipa District High School, living and working with Elwyn Richardson. He visits Oruaiti school to help with their pottery programme and builds their first kiln.

1961 Barry moves to Coromandel and spends two terms teaching at the high school as Art and Science teacher then he leaves teaching permanently and must pay off his bond of £300 to the Education Department. "I became a fulltime handcraft potter. I rented a villa in Coromandel, built a kiln and made some architectural 'star tiles' for the lift towers of a government building in Rotorua."

Barry Brickell, Helen Mason and Len Castle tutor at the 11th Adult Education Art and Design school. Barry exhibits at the Globe Theatre, Dunedin. His first exhibition as a fulltime potter.

1962 He moves house. "I rented a dilapidated old kauri villa in Top town, the upper and historic part of Coromandel township. Within a year I had made enough to put a deposit on the property valued at £1100... I got a shock at owning a property at 27 but I decided that this was my wife and family." Shirley Brickell and friends start the Devonport Festival Society to organise annual exhibitions of craft work.

Bernard Leach visits New Zealand and flies over to Coromandel to see Barry's new home. A film is made of Len Castle and Barry talking with Bernard Leach.

Barry exhibits at the NZSP sixth exhibition, at the art gallery, Palmerston North, in October. Also he is selected to be shown at the World Craft Exhibition at the NZ Embassy, Washington, USA. At The Playhouse Theatre, Dunedin, he exhibits mainly utility ware. He becomes friends with Dr Deirdre Airey.

1963 Barry is a founding member of the NZ Society of Potters, October 1963. He applies for and gets an Arts Council of NZ grant.

Barry Brickell's work is included in the NZSP seventh exhibition Otago Museum. He is included in the Australia/NZ Pottery exhibition touring Australian state galleries 1963/4 and is also in an exhibition at New Vision showing the first of a whole new range of work, sculptural, domestic and garden wares.

Jeff Scholes pots with Barry and most of the first Driving Creek Railway is built. Michael Illingworth stays at DCR for three months toward the end of 1963.

1964 The Arts Advisory Council tour New Zealand painting and ceramics to Japan,

Malaysia and India. They choose three Brickell pieces: a slab cube and pot worth 18 guineas; slab tower and pot unit of 15 gns (gns: 1 guinea is worth £1/1s), and three bridged bottles; all are stoneware.

Barry exhibits in the NZSP eighth exhibition, NZ Academy of Fine Arts, Wellington and some of his work is included in an exhibition at Aladdin's Gallery, Kings Cross Sydney.

1965 Barry exhibits at the Otago/Southland Potters first exhibition, OSB Chambers, Dunedin, June.

Shoji Hamada visits Christchurch and Barry joins other potters at Yvonne Rust's studio where he watches Hamada working.

At the New Vision Gallery, his first one-man exhibition *Barry Brickell* held in October 1965. Barry confesses that "As a child I was obsessed with fires and furnaces, earth, clay, native plants, rocks and old, heavy machinery, particularly steam engines and railways." There are two catalogues issued: one large and one small pamphlet.

He is in the NZSP ninth exhibition at AIM in November. Barry also exhibits at the Globe Theatre, Dunedin in April and at Several Arts Gallery, Christchurch. His work includes a whole range of thrown 'utility' ware including salt glazed crocks. The pots are transported to Dunedin in a hired railway wagon filled with straw.

1966 Yvonne Rust moves to Greymouth. Barry visits Toss and Edith Woollaston at Greymouth.

Exhibition at Centre Gallery, Wellington, in July. Barry is making large works, salt glazed, knob handled mugs, bread crocks, wine bottles, 'splodged' dinner plates.

8.10.1966 In the *Waikato Times* a full front page feature about 30-year-old Barry Brickell: 'Craftsman or Artist? — a potter finds peace in the Coromandel'. Barry has built a quarter of a mile of track on a 1 1/4 acre section. The 10 1/2-inch gauge railway transports clay and diesel oil to the kilns. Barry has just commissioned a small locomotive powered by an old Austin Seven Motor. "It's probably the smallest working railway in NZ" he says. Marti Friedlander photographs DCR.

At the New Vision Gallery is 'Barry Brickell', his second one-man exhibition of pottery 7-18 November; the result of three round kiln firings: large salt glazed, coal-fired pots. The pieces range from ashtrays to fatso jugs, crocks and tall planters, all salt glazed.

Barry is a founder member of the NZ Railway Preservation Society.

NZRPS rescue the C and CB locomotives from Mananui bush tramway.

1967 Barry features in the 12 New Zealand Potters calendar, a New Vision Production. He exhibits at the ASA NZ Pottery and Weaving exhibition, Auckland Festival and Exhibition Centre Gallery, Wellington. He visits the West Coast with Merv Smith and David Black. Barry builds a round coal-fired salt glaze kiln for Yvonne Rust near Greymouth.

1968 June/July: '11 + 1 invited Potters' at Palmerston North Art Gallery. New Vision Gallery Exhibition – salt glazed crocks. 'Little Paintings, Big Pots' by Michael Illingworth and Barry Brickell at Barry Lett Galleries in December.

Barry also exhibits at Stewart Dawson's Jewellers Dunedin and at the Display Centre, Wellington. Some Auckland schools have kilns designed and built by Barry.
He buys a truck to transport his pottery.

1969 At Peter McLeavey's Gallery, Wellington, Barry exhibits large pots.
Barry spends seven months with Yvonne Rust in Greymouth at her invitation making 'some of the best pots he had ever made'. While on the West Coast he gives a weekend workshop and helps other local potters. He revells in the superb clays available in the South Island. He works with the other members of the NZ Railway Preservation Society to rescue bush locomotives from remote mill sites in the King Country and on the West Coast. Bryce and Heather Stevens are caretaking at Driving Creek Railway.
September: Exhibition at Dawson's Gallery, Dunedin. At Peter McLeavey's Gallery, Wellington he exhibits West Coast welded scrap steel sculptures and salt glazed sculptural pieces. December finds Barry exhibiting in the New Vision Gallery Christmas exhibition of hand-woven rugs and pottery. Barry offers to sell a Colin McCahon watercolour to ACAG for $70. One of the *Towards Auckland* series.

1970 May: Barry begins a new coal-fired salt glaze kiln at the end of the railway line he built onto his neighbour Sid Savill's farm. He has four wagons and the locomotive 'DCR 167' on his track and would pull a wagon load of three large, vertically stacked shelves of wine bottles to be salt glazed.
September: exhibition at Dawson's Gallery, Dunedin. He is included in the W.C.C.N.Z. Asian Exhibition. Barry is guest exhibitor at the Auckland Studio Potters 8th Exhibition, at AIM in September. He is also guest exhibitor at the Mawhera Potters Exhibition.
Barry buys the launch *St Lawrence*, overhauls it and is caught in Cyclone Rosie.

1971 Barry finds and buys the *Presto*, a 75-year-old, triple skin kauri launch. She was originally a steam launch for the Auckland port doctor. He plans to refit her as a steam launch with a ketch-rig. Barry joins the Auckland Steam Engines Society.
Peter McLeavey Gallery, Wellington, Exhibition.

1972 At Dowse Art Gallery, Barry Brickell's 'Gourdal Column' exhibited in June.
Barry visits Australia to demonstrate moulding. He sells the launch *St Lawrence*.
July: Peter McLeavey's gallery shows pots by Brickell: A fleet of boats launched in the McLeavey show. It includes: *Bladders and bows, Bladdyl column*, salt glazed. *Pile of boats* and *Ironscape Coromandel* $300 as a sculpture.
September: New Plymouth. 'Columnar Peopillics' opened by Min. of Internal Affairs Mr Highet and Mrs N. Adams, the president of the New Plymouth Potters Group. It is a large exhibition of 179 works by 11 leading potters.
15th NZSP Exhibition at NZ Academy Gallery Oct/Nov.

1973 Barry makes voyages regularly from Coromandel to Auckland with his launch the *Presto*, delivering pots and returning with demolition building materials. He has plans to fit a new steam engine and ketch-rig sails to *Presto*.
"I decided to buy 60 acres of land. This became Driving Creek Railway." 1973 is given as the founding date for Driving Creek Narrow Gauge Railway.
Barry receives the Arts Council special project award 1973 for 'Development of Driving

Creek Potteries with utilisation and conservation of the resources of the land and sharing of work and ideas.' Wailin and Tom Elliott move into the house at the former property, now No. 90 Driving Creek Road. Barry retains his old room until his hut is built at the new site.

1974 17th National Potters Exhibition, AIM Oct/Nov. Barry is completely involved in building the new DCR. There he and his team build the first wood-fired stoneware kiln in NZ plus an oil-fired kiln and another wood-fired stoneware kiln. The firebox design follows the 'Dutch Oven' fireboxes of the old King Country steam boilers. Short of money, Barry sells his boat's diesel engine and later the *Presto* herself.

1975 18th National Potters Exhibition, AIM Oct/Nov. The railway was begun immediately to bring firewood and clay to the wood-fired kilns and pottery facilities. In 1975 Barry takes a five week long holiday in Dunedin with Ralph Hotere and builds him a kiln. Ralph convinces Barry of the importance of doing your own creative projects. Barry is included in the 10th Anniversary exhibition of Barry Lett Galleries; in CSA Gallery *The Group Show* — 75 and in *Light Terracotta,* an exhibition at the Dowse Art Gallery, Lower Hutt (the Dowse).

1976 It is reported that Barry Brickell plans to start a community of potters working together at DCR. He has stopped taking on apprentices. He wants to make the potteries economic. October NZSP 19th National Potters Exhibition, CSA gallery. Barry Brickell & Stanley Palmer show *Pots and Prints* at New Vision Gallery to 10 December: Variations on a Columnar theme in Terracotta.

1977 March-April: *Retrospective* at the Pofflatt Gallery, Pollen Street Thames. Easter: there is a potters' reunion at Parua Bay, Yvonne Rust's earth house situated on Whangarei Harbour. Barry writes "Many thanks to Yvonne for giving me the enforced relaxation and full tummy and opportunity for designing my house-to-be while sitting comfortably in your own new house which has finally and eventfully come to a splendid fruition." NZAFA Gallery, Wellington: 20th Exhibition of NZSP. Barry exhibits in the 'retrospective' as well as current sections. He exhibits at both the Bonython Art Gallery, Sydney and the New Vision Gallery Christmas Exhibition.

1978 A Brickell pot travelled as a part of the Dunedin Art Gallery's exhibition in Ashburton. He features as a craftsman teacher alongside Yvonne Rust in *Art in Schools*, a volume produced by the NZ Education Department. He has no fewer than seven other potters of various abilities living and working at DCR.

He features as a part of 'Ceramics in Progress', the work of 12 NZ Potters, Sarjeant Gallery, Wanganui. He comments that his ambitions are "To keep improving and fostering good craftsmanship and expression, making things which serve a human need." Barry is asked to represent New Zealand at the Craft Exposition at the Edmonton Commonwealth Games, by the Arts Council led by Hamish Keith. He is also included in the 'Craft NZ' touring exhibition, QEII Arts Council in tandem with the Ministry of Foreign Affairs. He spends three or four months exploring Canada and the USA. 'Potters' Doo' for a week in January at DCR. Barry changes his views about how he should operate the potteries.

1979 Barry exhibits at New Vision Gallery.

Max Gimblett, painter, an old friend of Barry's, visits from New York. Barry makes a set of 18 terracotta tiles for the Devonport Public Library.

NZSP 22nd National Exhibition at the Southland Museum, Invercargill.

1980 May: Barry designs the Waitaki NZ Refrigeration mural.

The Govett Brewster Art Gallery in New Plymouth commissions a full exhibition of Barry Brickell's work. This becomes 'Baroque Politocaust': Govett Brewster Art Gallery 6 to 21st Sept. It features 40 sculptured terracotta clay forms filled with steam in a setting of native plants. Barry's sister Andrea and her husband Robert Oliver play live baroque music. Barry meets John Matthews, engineer and businessman on the trustee board of the Govett Brewster. They become fast friends.

Barry's work included in the 'Then and Now' exhibition at the Dowse in May.

1981 February: Barry finishes the Waitaki project. In April Waitaki NZR celebrate their centenary with the commissioned timber framed, sculpted tile mural by Barry Brickell. It hangs in Waitaki's Head Office in Kilmore Street, Christchurch. QEII Arts Council advice was used to select the winning submission.

July: 'Torsomorphs or Torsic Growth Forms' at Wellington City Art Gallery. The sculptures had spent three years out in the open to grow layers of moss on them.

Maurice Brickell assists managing the finances of DCR.

Barry reports: "The railway has completed the spiral section, a full horseshoe curve climbing all the way and now racing around the hill above the potteries heading for the big pines."

Last Summer Doo at DCR — in the 'Snake Pit' a lot of raving went on in that time. "The teacher personality, the guru, is gone."

1982 Barry spends one month in Vanuatu setting up a pottery there to teach the local people how to fire pots. Two students come to New Zealand to learn more techniques. Included in *Clay Artists* exhibition at New Vision Gallery.

Exhibits as part of a group at the Ponsonby Community Centre.

Barry becomes interested in the story of Parihaka Pa in Taranaki and makes a memorial tile doorway for the Pa.

1983 Oct/Nov 25th Annual NZ Potters Exhibition, Govett Brewster Art Gallery, New Plymouth.

1984 July: Barry opens the TSB Craft Review at the Govett Brewster, New Plymouth. Exhibition New Vision Arts.

Barry is writing his book and is busy working on commissions. In October he completes mural for the foyer of the Shell BP Todd Oil services tower in New Plymouth. He is Guest Exhibitor at the 1984 Christchurch Festival Pottery Exhibition in the CSA Gallery.

1985 Launch of *A New Zealand Potter's Dictionary* by Barry Brickell (Reed Methuen $24.95). Peter Gibbs says of it "For the non-potter this is a book by the Barry Crump of NZ non-fiction."

14 Relief Tiles — *Stations of the Cross* Exhibition at Peter McLeavey's gallery. Barry has seven works in 'Treasures from the Land', a travelling exhibition in the USA. June-

August: 100 delegates visit DCR to spend a week salt glazing before attending the *Clay Az Art* international conference in Rotorua where Barry addresses the conference on the topic of coal-fired salt glazing.

Exhibits at the Dowse Art Museum.

1986 Barry is making "erotic" terracotta and other pots frequently now and working on and thinking about the commission he has received from John Matthews to make a series of terracotta erotic murals for a terracotta brick wall on John's property.

June: 'Coromandel Ikons': 14 *Stations of the Cross* exhibited at Wesley Chapel, Queen Street, Auckland.

Works exhibited at Dowse Art Museum.

Taupo Post Office mural.

June: After winning the Air New Zealand QEII Arts Council Travel Award Barry visits Helsinki specifically to attend a conference at the Arabia pottery. He will examine the relationship between their studio and industrial pottery, for which this factory is famous. Barry says Crown Lynn and Temuka potteries must be given credit for trying to heighten the quality of their product by establishing an involvement between studio potters and mass manufacturing.

He will also visit the University of Arizona's Ceramics Department which became intrigued with Barry's coal-fired salt glazing when he addressed the international *Clay Az Art* conference in Rotorua. Barry builds a salt glaze kiln at the University of Arizona's ceramics department and this inspires him to build a new salt glaze kiln at DCR. After Helsinki Barry goes north to Lapland then through Norway and Sweden to see the geological weathering of the granitic rocks there and to study wood carbonisation and by-product recovery.

Barry continues his journey in the UK, visiting the workshop of Kenneth Clark in Sussex. He explores Kent, Cornwall, parts of Wales and Scotland, much of it on bicycle. He also visits Spain.

1987 January: Barry attends the 'Summer Doo' Northland Craft Trust Whangarei. Helen Mason moves into DCR with her house truck. The launch *Ngaru* is loaned to Barry for long-term use.

Albany Village Pottery 'Barry Brickell' April 10-24th. Includes majolica pieces, a technique Barry rediscovered in Spain. He delivers the pots in *Ngaru* via the Albany Creek. 'Mined Out: Artists against Mining the Coromandel' exhibition at the Kitchener Gallery, Auckland. Sculpture *Doggoscape*.

Barry uses the *Ngaru* and every few months ships pots for sale to Auckland where he ties up at the wharf at the foot of Queen Street. The pots are sold at 43 Carbine Road Mt Wellington. This is called 'The Pot Place' and is run by Murray Norman, an old friend who would buy up whole kiln loads of Barry's domestic ware and sell them because he loves Barry's domestic ware.

May-June: 'Small Works for Growing Artists' at Nathan Homestead, Manurewa. Donated works are sold to benefit the Pacific Island Fine Arts Trust. The idea of Fatu Feu'u, a Mangere Lithographer.

31/12/87 Barry is in the New Year honours list, awarded an OBE for services to New Zealand Pottery and Ceramics.

1988 Driving Creek Railway runs passenger trains scheduled once per day at 5pm and is donation-only funded.

February: Work by Barry Brickell at the Pot Place, Auckland. Three times each year The Pot Place is organised by Murray Norman until 1990.

May: Over 100 native trees planted on Barry's property by the Coromandel branch of the Forest and Bird Society with Barry, Duncan Bayne, Megan Wilson and Peter Hills. Also in May: Barry is presented with his OBE at Government House, Wellington. The previous day his guardian dogs were unveiled at the National Library. He made six dogs before he got two acceptable ones. In the newspaper it is reported: "Mr Brickell said he wanted to capture in his creations the look which librarians seem to have. He used to know a librarian or two, he said. "They are so serious about life, particularly about silverfish." A video is made of the installation of the dogs.

1989 Barry announces in *Rails* magazine that his railway is now open to the public. The double-decker viaduct is planned and the foundations laid on 29 March. Engineer Nelson Valiant did the calculations and assisted with the design work.

June: TV One feature on the arts programme 'Kaleidoscope' *Fire, Steam and Clay* about Barry Brickell, directed by Peter Coates.

October: Barry is invited Guest Potter at Auckland Studio Potters 25th Annual Exhibition at AIM.

16 October the first train crosses the double-deck viaduct on the lower level.

Petra Meyboden makes 'DCR' slip decorated tiles as payment for studio space. Barry is involved in the anti-mining Save the Coromandel protests and writes to the Minister of Conservation. He features as part of the 'Pioneer Potters' exhibition, The Potter's Shop, Wellington Sept/Oct. Steve Scholfield and Barry build a double chamber salt glaze kiln at Driving Creek Potteries.

1990 George Sempagala, a Ugandan potter, works at DCP.

March: 'Celebration, Aspects of Contemporary NZ Art', an exhibition at the Fisher Gallery, Pakuranga. It also includes Phillipa Blair, Don Binney and Don Driver among others.

June: 'Railway Connection' exhibition by Gary Tricker and Barry Brickell featuring a model railway supplied by Manawatu Model Railway Club. Manawatu Art Gallery, Palmerston North.

Barry makes plans for the eventual ownership of DCR: The Queen Elizabeth National Trust will inherit the property on behalf of the nation.

October: Driving Creek Railway line is officially opened by the Mayor of Coromandel and fare paying commences.

November: Barry's work features in the 'Kiwiana' exhibition organised by the Crafts Council and curated by Jim & Mary Barr.

December: Barry exhibits pots and early drawings at the Joan Livingstone Gallery, Prince's Wharf, Auckland. This was the final 'Pot Place' exhibition with Murray Norman.

1991 May: Coromandel Potters at the Pumphouse, Takapuna. Barry is using a mix of washing soda and baking soda for salt glazing as it is less polluting. The double-deck viaduct is completed at Driving Creek Railway, an outstanding engineering achievement.

1992 Driving Creek Railway is mentioned by the travel columnist of the *Boston Globe* newspaper with glowing descriptions.

The Snake railcar completed, capacity 50 persons. The railway line is now almost 3km long, ending at Hoki Mai where BBQs are held in summer.

Barry is commissioned by the Maritime Museum for a work to commemorate the 350th anniversary of Tasman's sighting of New Zealand.

Commissioned by James Mack to make pieces about the Pacific/Spain for the Seville World expo. Other pieces displayed at Masterworks, Parnell in April-May.

'Resurrection of the Goddess', seven recent pots by Barry Brickell, December at Peter McLeavey Gallery.

1993 Barry finishes the *Heemskerk Galleon* as a commemoration of the 350th anniversary of the sighting of New Zealand by Abel Tasman.

April: 'Landform' exhibition, John Leech Gallery.

June: Some of Barry's older works for sale at Albany Village Gallery, .

September: 'Coromandel Calling' Aotea Centre, Auckland.

December: 'Noa Noa — to tie together' with Fatu Feu'u at the ASB Bank, Auckland. *Crossing cultural boundaries* reviving Lapita pottery found in Samoa. Fatu Feu'u scribed Polynesian patterns on nine of Barry's large sculptural coiled forms.

The Possum railcar completed.

1994 Brickell pots included in 'Function', a display of selected items from the Dowse Art Museum March-October.

A sculpture garden set up at DCR.

Barry prints a small book about the history of DCR, DCP and the Coromandel for the tourists who pass through DCR in droves every day.

Trains running frequently each day during summer months.

1995 21 January: Barry's studio burns down with the loss of many photographs and engineering drawings. Arson suspected .

Helen Mason is 80 years old.

Cascade switchback built and the Terminus reached in the railway construction, June. 26 October: Barry is 60 years old. 28 October, 'A Mild Celebration' at DCR & P. Special friends are invited "to attend the 60th anniversary of a 2-wheeled vertical boiler which has provided copious steams and pots during its installation at Devonport, Newmarket, Newton then Coromandel, over the past 40 years. Invited guests and other rolling stock may arrive with suitable fuel and tube-cleaner for a significant event full of steam, hot air and raves. Ash and clinker facilities available. Pots ranging from awful to beaut welcome subject to their being made of clay or iron, and not by politocrats."

1996 March: Publication of *Barry Brickell: A Head of Steam* by Christine Leov-Lealand in new series 'New Zealand Lives: The People Who Shaped The Nation'.

Appendix 2

Barry Brickell's Designs, Inventions and Pioneering Achievements.

1958 Testing many New Zealand ceramic raw materials for suitability as potters' materials for pottery, tiles and bricks.

1960 The 'train machine' musical instrument.

1962 Restoration (as opposed to modernisation) of old kauri villa.

1963 Native forest restoration in the Coromandel area.

1969 'Fun machines' made from scrap materials.

1974 The Dutch Oven firebox for wood-fired stoneware kilns.

1975 A railway that is environmentally friendly.

1984 Terracotta planters that are self-watering.

1986 The multi-flue wood-fired balanced updraught-downdraught kiln.

1987 Exposing the story of the ecological degradation of Coromandel since European settlement.

1991 The double-deck railway viaduct.

1992 The chain-driven, differential axle, every wheel driven every wheel braked railway bogie design.

Creating forms related to the Crown's actions (as distinct from pakeha actions) about Maori culture.

Original Driving Creek Railway.

Present Driving Creek Railway.

BIBLIOGRAPHY

Many *New Zealand Herald* articles over the years.

Hauraki Herald articles.

Art in Schools, 'The New Zealand Experience', School Publications Branch, Department of Education, Wellington, NZ 1978.

A New Zealand Potter's Dictionary, Barry Brickell, Reed Methuen Publishers Ltd 1985.

10 Years Of Pottery In New Zealand, Helen Mason, published by Helen Mason, 1968.

NZ Historic Places #41, May 1993 article by Barry Brickell about restoration of the kauri villa.

New Zealand Listener 20 Feb 1988, p.63: 'Pot Promotion' by Bill Lennox and other articles from various years.

Waikato Times, 8 Oct 1966. Front page feature article by Frank Nerny, photos by Brian Leach of Barry pushing 44 gallon drums with his small train, pouring from a teapot, throwing a large bowl. 'He is one of NZ's leading young potters.'

NZ Crafts, 11, Spring 1969; Barry member of QEII Arts Council.

NZ Potter 1970 Vol 12 No. 42 and many other references to Barry in *NZ Potter* magazine.

Accent ecumenical magazine, June 1986 article on pp.33-39 about Coromandel potters.

Art NZ several issues.

The Crane & the Kotuku — Artistic Bridges Between New Zealand and Japan by Dianne & Peter Beatson, Manawatu Art Gallery, 1994.

North And South, January 1992.

The Story of Driving Creek, Barry Brickell, 1994.

INDEX

About the author

Christine Leov-Lealand is descended from Nelson pioneer stock and lived for the first 10 years of her life on D'Urville Island in the Marlborough Sounds. She began writing early and gained a B.A. in History at Otago University in 1981. Christine has lived in many parts of New Zealand, has a daughter and cares for numerous stepchildren.

Since 1992 she has been writing, travelling and researching a biography of the artist Theo Schoon. As an oral historian Christine records life memories on tape and also writes poetry. She is writing a novel and continuing her research while sailing in Polynesia.

New Zealand Lives Series